PANCHAYATI RAJ in India

India–the Land and the People

PANCHAYATI RAJ in India

M. ASLAM

nbt.india
एकः सूते सकलम्

National Book Trust, India

ISBN 978-81-237-5188-7

First Edition 2007
Reprints 2010 (twice), 2011 (twice), 2014, 2015,
2019 (*Saka* 1941)

₹ 140.00

Published by the Director, National Book Trust, India
Nehru Bhawan, 5 Institutional Area, Phase-II
Vasant Kunj, New Delhi-110 070
Website: www.nbtindia.gov.in

Dedicated to elected members of Panchayats

Contents

FOREWORD

Panchayats—the rural local governments of our country—got Constitutional protection and sanctity only after the 73rd Amendment in 1993 which led to the incorporation of Part IX and IX A in the Indian Constitution. They have, of course, existed as institutions of local government since ancient times. However, their development as organised Institutions with codified rights and responsibilities has been uneven across the different States of the country, depending upon the political will of successive State Governments as 'local government' is a subject exclusively on the State List in our Constitution. The 73rd Amendment has given a new lease of life to these Institutions in their role as the third tier of our governance structure by mandating elections every five years and providing for reservation for women and socially deprived classes. The creation of a new Union Ministry of Panchayati Raj has helped focus on the strengthening and empowerment of these institutions across the country. The vision of Panchayats acting as institution of self government can only be realized if we work towards empowering Panchayats and their Gram Sabhas by devolving the three Fs—specific functions, commensurate finances and accountable functionaries to the Panchayats. This will help our rural populace to access their entitlements through empowerment, thus leading to their enrichment and going a long way towards addressing the concern for a more equitable model of growth for all our citizens.

The initiative of the author and the National Book Trust in bringing out an overview of Panchayati Raj in India is most welcome, as a significant portion of our educated citizenry is still unaware of the silent revolution taking place in our countryside through our Panchayats—not least of which is the empowerment of our traditionally disadvantaged communities and women through reservations for Panchayat seats.

Mani Shankar Aiyar
Union Minister of Panchayati Raj

New Delhi
March 2007

PREFACE

The local self-government, as a system, has existed in India since long. Its form may have varied, but its spirit has always been a part of our socio-cultural ethos. In the medieval times, it was seen in the form of a ***Gram Sabha*** functioning through its executive committee viz Panchayat, a village body able to govern and sustain small communities of people. During the British period, the institution became the instrument of the ruling elite, intended to project the interests of the British Government. After independence, it was in 1959 that the local self-government system, known as Panchayati Raj took its present shape. The enthusiasm generated by this new form of local self-government, however, did not last long. Conflicting interests at various levels eclipsed the concept as well as its practice. After decades of debate, the Constitutional (73rd Amendment) Act-1992 outlined the task of rejuvenating the Panchayati Raj system in the country.

The institution of Panchayati Raj is now recognised as an important mechanism for decentralizing power and ensuring people's participation in development activities. It received special emphasis after the 73rd Constitutional Amendment which made the transfer of power to the panchayats a part of the most basic document of this nation—**The Constitution of India**. We have come a long way. It is now about one and a half decades since the 73rd Constitutional Amendment came into effect. It is high time that we examined its historical evolution in its appropriate perspective and at the same time recognised and confronted directly the complexities and inherent paradoxes involved in materialising democratic decentralisation through Panchayati Raj. A large number of publications have appeared on the subject of Panchayati Raj during the last one and a half decades, but very few of these have been addressed to the elected representatives of Panchayats who are the ultimate engines of the process of democratic decentralisation. They need to know about its past, present and future.

It was also felt that an attempt should be made to locate photographs of those who contributed to the evolution of Panchayati Raj in India and those responsible for giving it its present shape. It was also realized that although a number of committees were constituted in the post-independence period to study its various aspects and to make reformative recommendations, the common people could not have access to the deliberations/reports of these committees.

This publication considers the various stages through which this system evolved and also the promise it holds for the future. Further, an attempt was made to locate photographs of historical importance and place them at appropriate places in the text. I sincerely acknowledge the sources from where they have been taken. The author was lucky to have access to the February 1989 issue of *Kurukshetra* which carried extracts from the reports of various committees on Panchayati Raj Institution. I am thankful to the Ministry of Rural Development, Government of India, for allowing me to print these extracts as annexures to the main text. I found them very valuable and felt that their content needs to be shared with all those who are involved in Panchayati Raj in India.

I am grateful to Shri Mani Shankar Aiyer, Minister for Panchayati Raj, Government of India for having shown faith in me by suggesting my name to the National Book Trust for preparing this publication. I record my thanks to

Prof. Bipan Chandra, Chairman, National Book Trust, for providing me with this opportunity to share my thoughts on this subject of national importance with the common people.

I am also thankful to Shri D. Bandyopadhyay, former Convenor, Task Force on Panchayats, Rajiv Gandhi Foundation, not only for encouraging me to prepare this publication, but also for allowing me to use materials published by the Task Force on Panchayats. I am also thankful to Dr George Mathew, Director, Institute of Social Sciences, New Delhi, for allowing me to use the academic resources of the institute.

I would have not been able to shape this publication without the help of Prof. B.N. Koul. He is a meticulous editor. Last but not the least, sincere thanks to my wife Mrs Nuzhat Aslam and my daughter Ms Benish Aslam for creating and maintaining a congenial atmosphere at home. I hope that readers in general and those involved in Panchayati Raj in particular will enjoy this publication.

M. Aslam
Professor of Rural Development

March, 2007
New Delhi

1

INTRODUCTION

The experiences of the past suggest that the Panchayati Raj System could be a very effective instrument in the process of devolving power to lower levels for materializing democratic decentralization through people's active participation. The basic philosophy behind this thinking is that the process of development gets accelerated as and when common people identify themselves as active partners in the process of development. Another school of thought advocated by Norman Uphoff[1] (1985) considers "creation of local capacity for resource mobilization and management in support of development programmes", as a principal concern for existence of institutions of local governance. Whatever the case, the grass roots level institutions of local governance are important instruments in the process of democratic decentralization. Experimentation with one or the other form of democratic decentralization has been going on for quite sometime in many developing countries of South and South-East Asia. It has shown mixed results.

In the context of India, particularly rural India, the Panchayats have been providing the institutional mechanism for such democratic decentralization. It is a well known fact that Panchayats in one form or the other have existed in India since long. The literature on the subject reveals that even in medieval ages, in spite of radical political changes, one or the other form of village local-self government existed. During the British rule, we witnessed, the emergence of local-self government as a direct projection of the ruling elite. After independence, although the draft Constitution of India did not make any mention of Panchayats, a mention was added in the final draft under Article 40 in the chapter on 'Directive Principles of State Policy'. It states, "The State should take steps to organise Village Panchayats and endow them with such powers and authority as may be necessary to enable them to function as units of self-government." This provision of the Constitution was primarily advisory and not taken seriously. Immediately after the independence the policy planners got engaged in experimenting with the Community Development Programme (CDP) for most of the 1950s. It was only in 1959, that the Panchayati Raj System came into existence in a formal way after the Study Team headed by Balwantrai Mehta expressed concern about the lack of popular participation in the Community Development Programme and made a strong plea for the **devolution of power to lower levels through Panchayati Raj.** The initial enthusiasm generated by this system, however, did not last long and it was subjected to rough weather wherever introduced. What followed in the subsequent decades were some sporadic and indifferent steps taken by some of the state governments to organise Panchayats, but they were invariably denied any meaningful powers and authority and, worst of all, the elections were seldom held at 5-year intervals as required. During the late 1970s the formation of the ***Asoka Mehta Committee*** as a possible way out to catalyze rural development through Panchayati Raj could not turn the tide.

During the 1980s, various committees were constituted to suggest measures which could be taken to revive the Panchayati Raj System in India. The G.V.K. Rao Committee commissioned in 1985 to look into administrative arrangements for rural development suggested devolution of powers and authority to the village panchayats. In 1986, the L.M. Singhvi Committee pleaded for the constitutional recognition of, apart from attaching great importance to, the Gram Sabha. The Sarkaria Commission on Centre-State relations recommended strengthening of panchayats financially and functionally. In 1989, the Congress Committee headed by V.N.Gadgil recommended a three-tier system, five years term and reservation for weaker sections.

After a great deal of debate through various committees for almost over three decades we reached the threshold of reactivating the Panchayati Raj System, this time armed with the Constitution (73rd Amendment) Act, 1992. This was followed by Conformity Acts passed by the State Governments and elections to panchayats were held throughout the country. As a result of this revolutionary legislation, we witnessed that about 3.4 million people were elected throughout the country to the three-tiers of local governance in the country. It included more than one million women, most of whom made it to these bodies for the first time.

Equitable and just social and economic development pre-supposes the active involvement of the vast majority of the people in the process of development itself. Although we may feel justly proud of our achievements in various fields, large majorities of our people, especially those in rural areas, are still not active participants in the process of development. The primary reason for this imbalance is that the grass-roots level democratic institutions do not have any significant role in determining the directions of development. The revival of the Panchayati Raj Institutions (PRIs) through the 73rd Amendment of the Constitution of India was to correct this imbalance and to endow PRIs with the strength and prestige associated with self-governance structures sanctified by the Constitution itself.

It is necessary to mention here that local self-government is a subject mentioned in the state list incorporated in Schedule VII of the Constitution. Thus, the state legislatures have the required authority to decide about the structure, organization, functions, finances and all other issues concerning the process of local self-governance. This was the reason why various sates adopted various types of PRIs—varied number of tiers, various names, different methods of elections to the different tiers, different powers and functions and different financial support systems, before the enactment of the 73rd Constitutional Amendment. The Constitution (73rd Amendment) Act-1992 has given constitutional status to the panchayats as institutions of self-government. It provides for certain mandatory provisions which were considered essential for bringing in uniformity and for the sustenance of these institutions. The amendment is an important landmark in the process of democratic decentralization, because it has given legal recognition to the three-tier system of governance with Panchayati Raj Institutions (PRIs) at the district, intermediary and village levels, except in those states where the population is less than 20 lakhs. For them a two-tier system is prescribed. It also expects states to devolve adequate powers, responsibilities and finances upon these bodies so as to enable them to function as effective institutions of self-governance and to prepare plans and implement schemes for economic development and social justice. The expectation is that it will help improve the *delivery of some of the public goods and services*. Basically the 73rd Amendment Act provides a basic frame-work for the decentralisation of powers and authorities to the Panchayats. It is the responsibility of states to give it a practical shape. And the states are expected to act in consonance with the spirit behind the 73rd Amendment for establishing a strong and viable system of local self-government in India.

About 14 years have passed since the enactment of the 73rd Constitutional Amendment and during this period elections have been held twice in most of the states. The process of democratic decentralization set in motion by this historic legislation was expected to be directed towards achieving the goal of self-governance by the people. "It implies that they have to be democratic in nature (through regular and mandatory elections) with allocated values, priorities, and policies and should have been able to adjudicate over conflicts under their jurisdiction."[2] What we find in its actual implementation is that while the mandatory provisions of the 73rd Amendment have been followed, the state legislations differ considerably as far as the devolution of powers and functions to the panchayats is concerned. Article 243G of the Act states, "Subject to the provisions of the Constitution, the legislature of a state may by law, endow the Panchayats with such powers and authority as may be necessary to enable them to function as institutions of self-government and such law may contain provisions for devolution of powers and responsibilities upon the panchayats at the appropriate level, subject to such conditions as may be specified therein, with respect to: (a) the preparation of plans for economic development and social justice; (b) the implementation of schemes for economic development and social justice as may be entrusted to them including those in relation to the matters listed in the Eleventh Schedule. "It appears that necessary amount of thought could not be given between the enactment of Seventy-third Constitutional Amendment and subsequent state legislations. It turned out to be a race for catching the deadline rather than realistic thinking. In most cases, some amendments were incorporated in the already existing State Acts to make them look, ostensibly in conformity with the Seventy-third Amendment."[3] A number of amendments brought about in various State Acts, over the last more than a decade now, have not succeeded in catching up with the spirit of self-governance embodied in the Amendment yet.

In the Eleventh Schedule, there are 29 items ranging from agriculture, minor irrigation, mining of minor minerals to small scale industries as the functional areas of Panchayati Raj Institutions (PRIs). The Schedule also mentions education, health, literacy and sports. The welfare activities of the weaker sections and the disabled are also expected to be under the jurisdiction of PRIs. The responsibilities of rural housing, drinking water, non-conventional energy, women and child development, family welfare, social forestry and khadi and village industries are all expected to be assigned to PRIs. It seems that the "Panchayati Raj Institutions (PRIs), in effect, on paper are expected to be entrusted with the entire burden of rural development that the national and state governments have failed to shoulder".[4] The 'Activity Mapping' did not receive any serious consideration so far. The experience of a decade and a half long post-Amendment period reveals that the 73rd Amendment in general and Article 243G in particular have not been implemented in letter and spirit. It seems that there is large scale overlapping of functions/areas of responsibilities among the three levels of PRIs on the one hand and between the PRIs and the state agencies on the other. The situation has been further complicated by the lack of the basic awareness regarding the Panchayati Raj system and how to carry out assigned responsibilities among most of the elected members of panchayats. "One point that was meant to be not negotiable was the concept of 'institution of self-government'. But it lost its identity in the legal verbiage. This has resulted in conceptual confusion."[5] Whatever the case may be, the fact remains that even after having been conferred constitutional status through the 73rd Amendment about a decade and a half back, the panchayats have not emerged as genuine institutions for participatory self-government.

There are a number of factors responsible for such a state of affairs. One of these factors, which contributes to the present situation also, is the lack of awareness about the concept, meaning and functioning of Panchayati Raj both in retrospect and prospect on the part of elected members of panchayats. We still lack a clear-cut training policy for capacity building, so badly needed to materialize the concept of democratic decentralization through Panchayati Raj. As a result, there is hardly any visible impact of the sporadic training interventions made by the mushroom growth of government and non-government training institutions. We have been generating a lot of literature on the subject of Panchayati Raj, highlighting at times isolated successes which do not get replicated later or elsewhere. Invariably this literature is not in the format suitable for and the language of a common man, we consume it among ourselves.

We have witnessed absence of preparedness stemming from a lack of knowledge and awareness on the part of elected members to shoulder new responsibilities. To overcome this issue, as a first step, it is not only necessary but also crucial that the elected members of the panchayats are adequately equipped with the knowledge and awareness about the concepts and practices of self-governance along with that of the mandatory provisions of the 73rd Amendment Act. This could also serve as resource material apart from its reinforcing and supplementing the on-going training and other activities focusing on the various aspects of the state specific acts and other details.

The present publication on 'Panchayati Raj in India' is a modest attempt to have a look at Panchayati Raj System in retrospect and prospect. It is basically meant for those who are responsible to materialize the concept of democratic decentralization through Panchayati Raj in the country. It briefly looks at the historical background, analyses post-independence period leading to the enactment of the Constitution (73rd Amendment) Act-1992, discusses its main features and the post-amendment scenario. Finally, it analyses Principles of Local Governance before concluding with some thoughts on 'Empowerment of Panchayats—A perspective'.

References

[1] Norman Uphoff, *Local Institutions and Decentralization for Development* in *Local Government Institutions and Resource Mobilization*, BARD, Comilla, Bangladesh 1985

[2] *Revitalisation of Panchayati Raj in India—Problems and Prospects*, Task Force on Panchayati Raj, Rajiv Gandhi Foundation, New Delhi 1997

[3] Ibid p.2

[4] ibid p.12

[5] ibid. p.2

2

PANCHAYATI RAJ INSTITUTIONS—A RETROSPECTIVE

History tells us that local Self-government, in one form or another has been in existence in the Indian sub-continent for centuries. The evolution of the Panchayati Raj System can be traced through three distinct periods:[1]

- **Pre-British Period**
- **British Period**
- **Post-Independence Period**

Pre-British period

The origin of the local government system can be traced to medieval ages where "community spirit" was the main force not only to keep village communities united but also help them to manage local affairs independently. Not only they are mentioned in the *Rigvedas*, there is also a definite evidence available of the existence of village *Sabhas and Samities (Assemblies or Councils)* and *Gramins (village leaders)* in *Vedas*...This ancient system of village democracy later took form of panchayats (assembly of 5 persons) to look after the affairs of the village with police and judicial powers. Custom and religion elevated them to sacred position of authority.[2] Sir Charles Metcalfe, the provisional Governor General of India (1835-36), characterized them as *small republics having nearly everything that they want within themselves and almost independent of any foreign relations. They seem to last where nothing else lasts. Dynasty after dynasty tumbles down; revolution succeeds to revolution; Hindoo, Pathan,*

Mogul, Mahrhatta, Sikh, English, are all masters in turn; but the village community remains the same.... This union of the village communities, each one forming a separate state in itself, has, I conceive, contributed more than any other cause to the preservation of the people of India through all the revolutions and changes which they have suffered, and is in a high degree conducive to their happiness, and to the enjoyment of a great portion of freedom and independence[3]. In the villages different sections of the community helped and depended on one another and this mutual dependence was reinforced by age-old customs and traditions. Mobility was limited and so were their needs and aspirations. Since most of the village communities were self-sufficient in their day-to-day needs, the system of self-governance helped them remain intact and self-contained. The village bodies provided a link with higher authorities on all matters affecting the villages.

Sir Charles Metcalfe

In other words, each village was a compact socio-economic and administrative unit with its full complement of public functionaries as servants of the village community, —rather than (those) of the Government. With the ***Sabha*** comprising the adult residents of the village, functioning through its executive committee, viz— ***panchayat,*** no village affair was considered beyond its purview.[4] Despite many of the political changes in cities and towns during the medieval period, the system of panchayats in the villages continued undisturbed. "Although under the Mughals their judicial powers were curtailed, local affairs remained unregulated from above and village officers and servants were answerable primarily to the panchayats." [5]

British period

During the British period, the local government system

passed through two distinct phases. The first phase commenced with from the advent of the British rule and lasted till the Constitutional Reform of 1919 and the second phase from 1919 to the end of the British rule.

First phase

During the first phase, the advent of the British rule saw the slow disappearance of the self-contained village local government system and the emergence of a local government as the direct projection of the British rule. They used this system to extend their own rule. As a result, the attitude of the people changed. People seemed to lose faith in the age old system of local government. Other conditions too had changed. Direct taxation gave way to indirect taxation. In many regions of the country, particularly in the North-Western provinces,—a leading or prominent person of their confidence was put in charge of various affairs including development and social welfare. This took the place of the local institutions like Panchayats. As Mathew rightly points out—*Village Panchayats were not the first priority of the British rulers. Concentrated as they were mainly around the trading centres, their interest in the beginning was limited to the creation of local bodies of nominated members in the major towns.*[6] The revolt of 1857 seems to have been largely responsible for creating the conditions for the adoption of Lord Mayo's resolution on local self-government reviving the traditional village panchayat system in Bengal. The transfer of authority to the local institutions, "was a financial necessity in the context of imperial financial strains and stresses in the wake of the mutiny," and that it called for, 'a comprehensive political philosophy involving the transfer of authority from the imperial level to the local representatives with legal, administrative and financial implications...'.[7]

Lord Ripon's Resolution (1882)

The report of the Famine Commission of 1880, pointing to the absence of institutionalized local bodies, as a major impediment in the process of bringing relief supplies to the affected people, further strengthened the case for the transfer of authority to local bodies. As a result in 1882, the Government of India Resolution on local self-government was announced. It envisaged a comprehensive geo-administrative country-wide principle for the local self-government institutions. "Lord Ripon's government sent circulars to the governments in the provinces on the subject of local self-government, in order to seek the popular, public opinion. The issues in the circular became the basis for the Government of India Resolution (1882). Then came into being The Local Bodies Act of 1885. This was the basis for setting up local self-governing institutions, but they had a majority of nominated members down to the village level."[8]

Lord Rippon

Royal Commission on Decentralization

Lord Ripon was liberal in his outlook towards the problem of local self-government. He thought the local self-governing institutions would act as instruments of political and popular education. Another major step in this direction was the report of the Royal Commission on Decentralization. This Commission was set up in 1907 and it submitted its report in 1909. The Commission recommended that it could be desirable for effective decentralization to associate people with local tasks and village affairs through the village panchayats. The commission recommended that, "it is most desirable, alike in the interests of decentralization and in order to associate the people with the local tasks of administration, that an attempt should be made to constitute and develop village panchayats for the administration of local village affairs."[9] Both the recommendations contained in the Ripon Resolution as well as those made by the Royal Commission on Decentralization, were not implemented and remained on paper only.

1909 Lahore Resolution

In 1909, the 24th Session of the Congress was held at Lahore. It adopted a resolution urging the Government to take early steps to have elected local bodies from village panchayat upwards with elected non-official chairmen for the local bodies and to provide them with necessary financial support. But all these efforts remained largely, on papers.

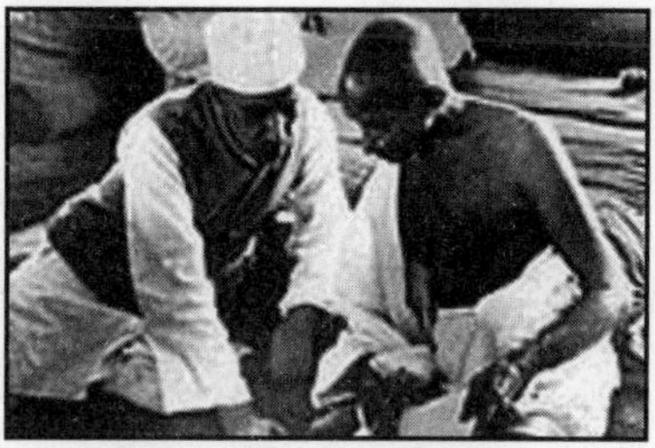

Congress in Session in 1942

Second phase

During the second phase various reforms were introduced largely as a consequence directed result of the developments that characterized from the first phase. The Montagu-Chelmsford Reforms of 1919, under the proposed scheme of dyarchy, made local self-government *a transferred subject*. This meant that local self-government was brought under the control of Indian Ministers in the provinces. The idea was to make the local bodies representative with popular control. However, it did not make the panchayat institutions truly democratic because of various constraints. A large number of Acts, however, were passed for the establishment of village panchayats, almost in all provinces, in order to fulfil the condition of transferring *this subject* to the domain of Indian Ministers in the provinces.

These included "Bengal Village Self-Government Act of 1919, Madras, Bombay and United Provinces Village Panchayat Act of 1920, Bihar and Orissa Village Administration Act, Assam Rural Self-Government Act of 1926, and Punjab Village Panchayat Act of 1935, etc".[10]

'In subsequent years, similar laws were adopted by some other states. These were—Bikaner (Village Panchayat Act, 1939), Karauli (Village Panchayat Act, 1939), Hyderabad (Village Panchayat Act, 1940), Mewar (Gram Panchayat Act, 1940), Jasdan (Village Panchayat Act, 1942), Bhavnagar (Village Panchayat Act, 1943), Porbandar (Village Panchayat Act, 1943), Bharatpur (Village Panchayat Act, 1944), Marwar (Gram Panchayat Act, 1945), Wadia (Village Panchayat Act, 1946), Dharangadhra (Village Panchayat Act, 1946), Morvi (Village Panchayat Act, 1946), Sirohi (Village Panchayat Act, 1947), and Jaipur (Village Panchayat Act, 1948). However, these statutory panchayats covered only a limited number of villages and had, generally, a limited number of functions.[11] These Acts aimed at looking after the village affairs and their development only. The local self-government even had the powers to try minor cases also. But these bodies were not democratic in the real sense because most of their members were not elected but were nominated by the government. They had few powers given to them and their

Mahatma Gandhi

financial resources were also limited. It was the time when Gandhi Ji categorically defined his vision of village panchayat thus—*My idea of village Swaraj is that it is a complete republic independent of its neighbours for its own vital wants and yet interdependent for many others in which dependence is a necessity... The Government of the village will be conducted by the panchayats of five persons annually elected by the adult villagers, males and females, possessing minimum prescribed qualifications. These will have all the authority and jurisdiction required. Since there will be no system of punishment in the accepted sense, the panchayats will be the legislature, judiciary and executive combined to operate for its year of office. Any village can become such a republic today without much interference even from the present government whose sole effective connection with the villages is the execution of village revenue... Here there is perfect democracy based upon individual freedom. The individual is the architect of his own Government.*[12]

Although the last few decades of the British rule witnessed a large number of state acts being passed for the establishment of village panchayats, the situation remained more or less the same till India achieved her independence.

Post-Independence period

All through the freedom struggle, the Indian National Congress perceived the Panchayats as people's institutions. Local self-governance was seen as the true voice of democracy. Village Panchayats were central to the ideological framework of India's national movement. Many of our leaders, mainly Mahatma Gandhi were wedded to the concept of *Gram Swaraj*. The idea was to have democratic process operating at the grass roots level as much as at the state and national levels. However, all this could not be translated into action, when India got her independence.

Article-40 'Organisation of Village Panchayats'

It is what Mathew (1994) calls a 'sad commentary on India's national commitment to democratic decentralization that despite the village, having a history as the basic unit of administration and despite the nationalist movement's commitment to panchayats and Gandhi Ji's unequivocal propagation of the ideal, the first draft of India's Constitution did not include a provision for panchayats.'[13] This was in spite of the fact that *Gram Swaraj (village self-rule)* was a major slogan in the national liberation movement. It is unfortunate that ***the*** founding fathers of our Constitution did not take notice of these facts, while preparing the first draft of the Constitution.

It is said that, 'When Gandhi Ji came to know about it, he felt both disturbed and depressed'. Rightly so, because 'Gram Swaraj' was the post-independence model of governance in rural India that Gandhi Ji had dreamt of. "Presumably, noticing his distress, an amendment was moved for inserting Article 40—Organization of Village Panchayats in Part IV of the Constitution–Directive Principles of State Policy."[14] Article 40 reads, T*he state should take steps to organize village panchayats and endow them with such power and authority as may be necessary to enable them to function as units of self-government.* This provision of the Constitution was primarily advisory in nature and therefore not taken seriously both by the Central and the State Governments. It is a fact that the Indian State, immediately after attaining independence, was more committed to industrialization and rural transformation through economic growth than democratic decentralization through Panchayati Raj. As a result, what followed was not an effort to usher in Panchayati Raj in the country, but to bring about socio-economic transformation through the 'Community Development Programme (CDP)',—a bureaucratically controlled state funded development intervention.

The First Development Initiative—CDP

The introduction of Community Development Programme (CDP) in 1952 with people's participation as its central concern was thus conceived as an instrument to transform the social and economic life of the village community. Right from the beginning, the programme was blown out of proportion as one of the most beneficent revolutions (Toynbee) and one of the major experiments of the 20th century (UN Mission). The CDP was soon strengthened by a National Extension Service to tackle the problems of growth and development at different local and functional levels. Even this could invoke only token public participation. It is, however, true that CDP was the first comprehensive programme for socio-economic transformation of rural areas. It is also a fact that it succeeded in establishing, for the first time, an organized administrative set-up at the national, state, district and block levels for the implementation of development programmes. It is equally true that the objective of self-reliance and people's participation could not be achieved through CDP, as it did not pay adequate attention to the objective of developing responsible and responsive leadership. The CDP followed a 'top-down' approach; thus, there was, relatively speaking, only token public participation effected through nominated representatives of the public.

The programme raised immense expectations. The expectations so raised could, however, not be fulfilled. There was also a lack of enthusiasm among people in the Community Development Programme because of the non-association of the people, particularly the disadvantaged rural poor and their representatives, in the planning and execution of development schemes meant for them. The people were not sufficiently motivated and there was a lack of strong commitment to the interests of the people among the inadequately trained development workers. As a result, dependence of the people on the Government for material resources continued and self help did not take roots at the expected level [15]. People continued to ask the Government for material resources.

Although, there were a few states like Rajasthan which introduced Panchayati Raj System as early as 1953 by enacting Rajasthan Panchayat Act—1953, "variations in terms of shape, formal legal status of the panchayats were so wide in different States that the need for systematic effort to usher in panchayati raj in the whole country, on more or less uniform basis, was greatly felt."[16] The lack of envisaged people's participation in CDP coupled with the lack of coordination constrained realization of the objective of self-reliance. There was a growing feeling among the policy makers that the development schemes would perhaps work only if the masses participated in them. It became increasingly self-evident that socio-economic transformation could not be achieved without democratic participation. Thus a study team on Community Projects and National Extension Service was set up in January, 1957 to assess the situation and to make necessary recommendations.

Birth of the Panchayati Raj System in Independent India

The Study Team on 'Community Projects and National Extension Service' headed by Balvantrai G. Mehta was set-up in January, 1957. In its report the Study Team observed that—"Development cannot progress without responsibility and power. Community Development can be real only when the community understands its problems; realizes its responsibilities; exercises the necessary powers through its chosen representatives and maintains a constant and intelligent vigilance on local administration."[17] It will be pertinent here to refer to some of the observations made by the Study Team in its report, which are relevant even today. On the state of resources the report states that, "one of the most important reasons for comparative lack of success of our non-urban local self-governing bodies is their exceedingly limited and inelastic resources." Similarly, on the role of panchayat samities the report mentions that, "the establishment of the panchayat samities with a wide devolution of power by the State Government has to be an act of faith—faith in democracy."[18] The team expressed concern about the lack of popular participation in the Community Development Programme and made a strong plea for establishing elected local bodies as soon as possible and for the devolution of power to lower levels through Panchayati Raj. Basic principles suggested by Mehta team were[19]:

- it should be a 3-tier structure from village to the district bodies having organic linkage with each other;
- there should be genuine transfer of power and responsibility to them;
- adequate resources should be transferred to the new bodies to enable them to discharge their responsibilities;
- all development plans/programmes at these levels should be channeled through these bodies;
- the system evolved should be such as will facilitate further devolution and transfer of powers and responsibilities in future; and .
- the higher level body, the Zilla Parishad, would play an advisory role.

The Planners and policy makers realized that the development efforts in rural areas could be fruitful only if the development strategy is based on invoking people's participation through panchayats as recommended by the Study Team. The Study Team report aptly sums up its findings in the following words—"Development cannot progress without responsibility and power. Community Development can be real only when the community understands its problems, realizes its responsibilities, exercises the necessary powers through its chosen representatives and maintains a constant and intelligent vigilance on local administration. With this objective, we recommend an early establishment of statutory elective local bodies and devolution to them of the necessary resources, power and authority."[20] Thus, the post-independence Panchayati Raj System formally came into existence in 1959 with two basic objectives. These were (a) democratic decentralisation and (b) local participation in planned programmes. The Balwantrai Mehta Committee recommended a three-tier system of Panchayati Raj. In other words, the system was to function at three levels, namely—district level (zilla parishad), intermediate level (block samiti) and lower level (village panchayat). The Committee suggested the setting up of Block Level Committees of elected representatives with adequate powers and resources for development programmes. The Team felt that in this way Panchayati Raj System would be able to establish a link between the people and the Government. Thus, after independence, India took more than a decade after independence for the Indian state to recognize the need for resurrecting the Panchayati Raj System.

Rise of Panchayati Raj (1959-64)

The states of Rajasthan and Andhra Pradesh were the first to adopt this system. On the occasion of lighting the lamp for introducing Panchayarti Raj System in the country on

2nd October, 1959 at Nagaur, in Rajasthan, Pt. Jawaharlal Nehru hailed it as "the most revolutionary and historical step in the context of new India" and remarked: "The reason for our slow progress is our dependence on official machinery". His concluding remarks were that "The time has come when the responsibility for planning and executing development schemes should be entrusted to the people. I am fully confident that in every part of India where responsibility is entrusted to the people, it will yield happy results." At some other occasions he further expressed that "Panchayati Raj is the 'real Swaraj' of the people. As we put our faith in our people, so will they respond and help in building up this great country of ours."[21] The speech given by the first Prime Minister of India, on what has been termed as *laying the foundation of democracy,* provides the necessary framework which was expected to be provided to the local self-government in independent India. Its excerpts are given at Annexure-I.

Pt. Jawahar Lal Nehru

By 1959, all the states had passed Panchayat Acts, and subsequently panchayats were set up in all parts of the country. "More than 2,17,300 village panchayats, covering over 96 per cent of the 5,79,000 inhabited villages and 92 per cent of the rural population had been established. On an average, a panchayat covered a population of about 2,400 in two to three villages. There were 4526 Panchayat Samities at the Block/Tehsil level covering 88 per cent of the blocks in the country. On an average a Panchayat Samiti covered about 48 Gram Panchayats. There were 330 Zila Parishads covering about 76 per cent of the districts in the country and each Zila Parishad had on an average 13-14 Panchayat Samities and about 660 Gram Panchayats."[22]

No doubt it was an impressive beginning. "There was a lot of enthusiasm generated in rural India and the people started feeling that they could have a say in affairs affecting their daily lives. Those were the promising days of Panchayati Raj Institutions in India"[23]. Thus the period between 1959-64 (some call it Nehru...S.K. Day period) was a period of Ascendancy as far as the Panchayati Raj System in India is concerned.

Stagnation and decline (1965-77)

Unfortunately this enthusiasm could not be sustained as it did not develop the requisite democratic momentum and failed to cater to the needs of rural development. The system was faced with several problems. These among others included i) change in development priorities, ii) lack of clarity about the concept of local self-government, iii) lack of funds, iv) the Panchayati Raj System adopted by the various states was not uniform, and v) political and bureaucratic resistance at the state level to the sharing of power and resources with the local level institutions. One explanation given is that "strengthening of local government institutions and adoption of community development approach did not go hand in hand with adequate delegation and devolution of powers, particularly in respect of planning and administration".[24] On the other hand, national development planners were busy experimenting with other development initiatives, like Green Revolution in the 1960s and Target Group Approach in the 1970s. This was partly due to their anxiety to show overnight results in food situation and partly to reach target groups to contain poverty. As a result, the Panchayati Raj system passed through a period of stagnation between 1965 and 1969 and went through a phase of decline from 1969 to 1977. It seems that perhaps power holders were not ready to share power with people. With the possible exception of Maharashtra, Gujarat, Karnataka and West Bengal, elsewhere these institutions were either superseded or allowed very little freedom to operate, which inevitably led to their decline.[25] As a result, local self-government system nourished through history and promised through the Constitution of India started languishing. It was only when development planners again realized that community participation in development planning was not forthcoming on expected lines and the poverty situation was showing little signs of recovery that they started looking back at local self-government through Panchayati Raj during the late 1970s as a possible way out to catalyze rural development. With the change of government at the national level in 1977, Asoka Mehta Committee was constituted to have a fresh look at the Panchayati Raj System.[26]

Asoka Mehta Committee

Thus the appointment of ***Asoka Mehta Committee*** in 1977 marked a turning point in the growth of Panchayati Raj[27]. It recognized the importance of the recommendations of earlier committees and reviews undertaken and clearly defined its focus stating that "India has gathered wide experience in the practice of democratic decentralization in the wake of recommendations of Balwantrai Mehta Study Team. The extent and form of democratic decentralization have varied from state to state and there have been ups and downs in the earnestness with which the programme has been pursued. The task of reviewing and assessing developments over the past decade and half is greatly facilitated by the valuable evaluations made by expert committees appointed by the different state governments

Asoka Mehta

and the Government of India from time to time. A voluminous literature has grown upon the subject. It would, therefore, not be necessary to cover the ground again. We need to confine ourselves to the main lessons the past experience has to teach and draw upon them for the future of Panchayati Raj."[28] The committee, after a comprehensive review of the literature and the situation, provided a definite philosophical treatment to the Panchayati Raj System. On the performance of Panchayati Raj during 1959-1977, the Committee observes: "The story of Panchayati Raj has been a story of ups and downs. It seems to have passed through three phases—the phase of ascendancy (1959-1964); the phase of stagnation (1965-69) and the phase of decline (1969-1977)."[29] It observed that rural India was the backbone of all development programmes. The future of India would depend on the welfare of the villages. Panchayati Raj as a system should contribute to the philosophy and functions of rural life in India. In its report the Committee listed several factors for the decline of Panchayati Raj. They included:[30]

i) **Disassociation of the programmes of development with the Panchayati Raj:** The report observed that, "The will for strengthening the PRIs further weakened with the demand of development programmes being kept out of its orbit becoming stronger."

ii) **Role of Bureaucracy**: On the role of bureaucracy, the report commented: "The bureaucracy has probably its own role in dissociating the PRIs from the development process—the officers would feel that they are primarily accountable for results and financial proprieties to the state government—they would, on the other hand, therefore, be averse to PRIs being entrusted with additional functions and on the other hand not easily get adjusted to working under the supervision of elected representatives."

iii) **Lack of Conceptual Clarity**: The report stated that, "Worst of all, there was lack of clarity in regard to the concept of Panchayati Raj itself and the objectives for which it should stand. Some would treat it just an administrative agency; others as extension of democracy at the grass roots level; and still others as a charter of rural local government."

iv) **Lack of Political Will:** The Committee observed that "an overview of the national scene would indicate that the activities of the PRIs were meager, their resource base weak and the overall attention given to them niggardly. The functioning of Panchayati Raj System thus became discouraging." It was felt that lack of political will to foster these institutions weakened the entire system.

v) **Disillusionment**: On working of PRIs and political interferences, the report of the committee observes: "In general, there has been disappointment with the working of PRIs which is traced, in stronger or milder terms, to a number of inadequacies and failure. PRIs are dominated by economically or socially privileged sections of society and have as such facilitated the emergence of oligarchic forces yielding no benefits to weaker sections. The performance of PRIs has also been vitiated by political factionalism, rendering developmental thrusts either warped or diluted. Corruption, inefficiency, scant regard for procedures, political interference in day-to-day administration, parochial loyalties, motivated actions, power concentration instead of service consciousness—all these have seriously limited the utility of Panchayati Raj for the average villager."

The main recommendations of the Committee were the following:[31]

- The district should be the first point of

decentralization under popular supervision below the state level. Below the district there should be *Mandal Panchayats* comprising a group of villages with a total population of 15,000 to 20,000. The Block level *Panchayat Samities* should be converted into non- statutory executive committees of *Zila Parishad,* and most of their functions would be taken up by *Mandal Panchayats* when the latter becomes active. At the village level, the people would be involved in *Mandal Panchayats* through Village Committees which would look after municipal functions and the related welfare activities.

- Election to Panchayati Raj bodies should be conducted by the Chief Election Officer of the State in consultation with the Chief Election Commissioner. Political parties should be allowed to participate in the elections as it would "facilitate healthier linkages with higher level political process."
- With the district as the strategic level for economic planning, the *Zilla Parishad* should be made responsible for planning at the district level. A professionally qualified team should be stationed at the district level for the preparation of district plans.
- The *Zilla Parishad* should consist of six types of members viz members elected from suitably demarcated electoral divisions, Presidents of *Panchayat Samities* as ex-officio members, nominees of bigger municipalities, nominees of district level cooperative federation, two women who get the highest number of votes in the *Zilla Parishad* elections and two co-opted members—one who is specially interested in rural development and the other drawn from University/College teachers.

- All the development functions relating to a district would have to be placed under the *Zilla Parishad*. Some of the functions which could be so decentralized include agriculture and allied sectors, health, education, communications, rural industries, marketing, welfare of backward classes, family welfare, etc.
- *Mandal Panchayats* would be responsible for implementation of schemes and projects assigned by the *Zilla Parishad*.

The most significant recommendation of the Committee was the two-tier Panchayati Raj System. According to this recommendation, the Zilla Parishad at the district level was to be established as the first point of decentralisation. It recommended the formation of Mandal Panchayats. A Mandal Panchayat was conceived to cover a group of villages, which would make necessary links with the system in developing focal points. It was also expected to develop links between rural and urban areas. One major weakness of the Asoka Mehta Committee was that it ignored the importance of the Gram Sabha.[32] In order that the weaker sections of society could derive maximum benefits from the various plans, the committee suggested that "there should be an independent authority to carry out 'Social Audit' of the funds and programmes earmarked for the Scheduled Castes and Scheduled Tribes and ensure that the projects designed for them are implemented in a way that the desired impact is not diluted."

The states of Karnataka, Andhra Pradesh and West Bengal passed new legislation based on the Committee's Report. Even though the experiences of Karnataka and Bengal were encouraging there was hardly any follow up at the Central level. The Chief Ministers' Conference in 1979 rejected the idea of two-tier system and favoured the continuation of the three-tier system.

G.V.K. Rao Committee

The G.V. K Rao Committee was set up in March, 1985 by the Planning Commission[33] to review the then existing administrative arrangements for rural development and poverty alleviation programmes, and to recommend appropriate structural mechanism to ensure that they are planned in an integrated manner and implemented effectively. The terms of reference of the committee, among other things included the study of the role of Panchayati Raj Bodies and their relationship with the proposed administrative set up, and to make appropriate recommendations in this regard. The Committee noted—"States have been generally lukewarm to the process of democratic decentralization. In most States the Panchayati Raj bodies have been allowed to languish without powers and resources. The Committee is of the opinion that there should be a significant decentralization at the District level."[34] The major recommendations of this committee were:[35, 36]

a) The Committee felt that the time had come to take a total view of Rural Development, so that it encompasses all economic and social development activities handled by different agencies at the field level;
b) Panchayati Raj Institutions have to be activated and given all support needed so that they can become effective organizations for handling people's problems. Elections to these bodies should be held regularly;
c) The district should be the basic unit for policy planning and programme implementation. The *Zilla Parishad* should, therefore, become the principal body for the management of all development programmes that could be handled at that level;
d) Panchayati Raj Institutions at the district level and below should be assigned an important role in respect

of planning, implementation and monitoring of rural development programmes;

e) Some of the planning functions at the state level might have to be transferred to the district level for effective decentralized district planning.

The Committee felt that the *Zilla Parishads* may operate through various committees. In order to ensure participation of all the members of the *Zilla Parishad* in one or the other committee, the members of the committee should be elected by members of the *Zilla Parishad* from among themselves in accordance with the system of proportional representation. The Committee believed that development would begin and continue, only if a large number of people participated. In order to achieve this, adequate powers and financial resources at the local level were considered essential. The Committee also felt that the block development office should be the spinal cord of the rural development process and that elections of local bodies should be held regularly.

L.M. Singhvi Committee

The Government of India set up a committee in June, 1986 headed by Dr. L.M. Singhvi to prepare a concept paper on the revitalization of the Panchayati Raj Institutions. The Committee felt that the Concept of Panchayats was a part of the philosophy of *Purna Swaraj* and *Gram Swaraj*. It considered Panchayati Raj Institutions as basic units of self-government. The Committee was of the view that, " It has been a fundamental error to regard Panchayati Raj Institutions primarily as convenient tools for administrative programmes and development projects. That error had the effect, in greater or lesser measure, of devaluing and

Dr L.M. Singhvi

downgrading the role of these institutions as units of self-government and relegating them to a secondary position, harming and hampering both democracy and development."[37] The Committee believed that the concept of Panchayati Raj Institutions must draw its inspiration from the quintessential concept of Gram Swaraj. This according to the committee is the explicit mandate and background of Article 40 of the Constitution. The Committee was of the view that the concept of village panchayats as units of self-government is central and integral to the Constitutional mandate and is vital in terms of the living rural reality. The Committee attached a lot of importance to Gram Sabha and considerered it as the embodiment of direct democracy.[38] Some of its major recommendations were:

- Local self-government should be constitutionally recognized, protected and preserved by the inclusion of a new chapter in the Constitution. Local self-government and more particularly, Panchayati Raj Institutions should be constitutionally proclaimed as the third-tier of Government.
- Elections to the Panchayati Raj bodies should be held promptly at the end of the specified term. A Constitutional provision should be made to ensure regular, free and fair elections for Panchayati Raj bodies and the task should be entrusted to the Election Commission of India operating through State Commissions or similar apparatus. No Panchayati Raj Institution should be allowed to remain superseded for more than six or seven months.
- In order to avoid apprehensions and charges of political bias or interference, the Committee recommended that Panchayati Raj Judicial Tribunal should be set up in every state to adjudicate

controversies in relation to elections, suspensions, supersessions, dissolutions and other matters relating to the working of Panchayati Raj Institutions and their elected personnel.

- Ways and means should be found to ensure availability of adequate financial resources for Panchayati Raj Institutions to function effectively. The Committee suggested that the Finance Commission appointed by the Union Government under the Constitution should make an adequate earmarked provision for Panchayati Raj Institutions.
- Participation of individuals attached to political parties should be discouraged. The Committee noted that it is neither practicable nor desirable to injunct the participation of individuals associated with political parties in Panchayati Raj Institutions by law.
- The Nyaya Panchayat should be given the functions of mediation and conciliation in addition to adjudication. The Committee was of the view that the institution of Nyaya Panchayats is a valuable aid to the development of social habits of self-government and rule of law. It suggested that there may be a Nyaya Panchayat for a cluster of villages constituted by election or appointed from a special panel to be prepared for the purpose.

The Committee was of the view that substantial training, research and public education inputs should be provided to strengthen the Panchayati Raj Institutions and the performance capabilities of those who are called upon to function as voters, elected representatives, administrative officials and voluntary workers in relation to Panchayati Raj Institutions. It felt that this would be the most productive and profitable investment in the process of building democratic institutions. It recommended that a model legislation within the framework of the proposed new chapter in the Constitution should be prepared with sufficient scope for appropriate local adaptations.[39]

Sarkaria Commission (1988)

The Sarkaria Commission, which was primarily concerned with the **centre-state relationship,** also recommended the strengthening of local bodies financially and functionally. The commission also believed that regular elections of Panchayats must be held. 'A notable recommendation was the creation of a body akin to the Finance Commission at the State level for devolution or transfer of resources to the districts on an operational and objective basis.'[40]

Other Committees

By the end of 1988, a sub-committee of the Consultative Committee of Parliament under the chairmanship of P.K. Thungon made recommendations for strengthening the Panchayati Raj system. One of its important recommendations was that Panchayati Raj bodies should be recognised constitutionally.

Similarly, a Congress Committee headed by V.N. Gadgil was set up in 1989. The committee recommended a three-tier system of Ranchayati Raj, a fixed term of 5 years and reservation for Scheduled Castes/Tribes and women. These recommendations became the basis for drafting the constitutional amendment bill.

V.N. Gadgil

Milestones in the Evolution of Local Government since Independence are given in Annexure-II.

References

[1] Aslam.M, *Local Self-Govt. in India- A Retrospect & Prospect in Federal*

India—A Design for Good Governance—Manak Publications, New Delhi 2005.

[2] Panchayati Raj in Rajasthan- Report- Seventh, (March -2001) Administrative Reform Commission, Department of Administrative Reforms, Govt. of Rajasthan.

[3] Dewey, Clive 1972. *Images of the village community: a study in Anglo-Indian thought. Modern Asian Studies* 6 (3).

[4] Multtalib, M.A. *Decentralisation, Local Government Institutions and Resource Mobilisation* edited by Hasnat Abdul Hye. BARD, Comilla, 1985. p.174.

[5] George Mathew, Ed. (1995) *Status of Panchayati Raj in the States of India-1994*, Institute of Social Sciences, Concept Publishing Company, New Delhi. p.1.

[6] ibid p.2.

[7] Multtalib, 1985 op. cit p.174.

[8] Aslam M. & Singh R.P. 1995, *Evolution of Panchayati Raj and the Constitutional (73rd Amendment) Act, 1992* in Panchayati Raj—The Context, Panchayati Raj Project material, IGNOU, New Delhi.

[9] Malaviya, H.D, (1965) *Village Panchayats in India,* Economic and Political Research Department, All India Congress Committee, New Delhi p. 258.

[10] Aslam op. cit

[11] George Mathew, Ed. (1995) op. cit p. 3.

[12] M.K. Gandhi, *My Idea of Village Swaraj*, Harijan, 26 July, 1942 in George Mathew's *Status of Panchayati Raj in the States of India 1994,* ibid p.4

[13] Mathew op. cit p.4

[14] Bandyopadhyay. D, (2004) *Panchayats and Democracy in New Issues in Panchayati Raj,* Task Force on Panchayati Raj, Rajiv Gandhi Foundation- Concept Publishing House, New Delhi p.147

[15] Aslam M. Decentralisation and Development Effort, *The Hindu,* May 24, 1994.

[16] Panchayati Raj in Rajasthan op. cit p.13.

[17] GOI, 1957. *Committee on plan projects: study team (Chairman: Balwantrai, G. Mehta).* New Delhi, Planning Commission, Government of India.

[18] Panchayati Raj: concept and approach, Extract from Reports of various Committees on PRIs—Balvantrai Mehta Committee, *Kurukshetra,* Vol.XXXVII No.5, February, 1989.

[19] ibid.

[20] ibid p.38.

[21] Panchayati Raj in Rajasthan- Op. cit p.14.

[22] *Kurukshetra* February, 1989 op. cit p.33.

[23] Mathew, George (Ed.) 1995, *Status of Panchayati Raj in the states of India*– 1994, ISS, Concept, New Delhi

[24] Hye, Hasnat Abdul, (Ed.) 1985, Decentralization, Local Government Institutions & Resource Mobilization. BARD, Bangladesh.

[25] Planning at Grassroots Level: An Action Programme for the Eleventh Five Year Plan—Report of the Expert Group, Ministry of Panchayati Raj, March 2006 New Delhi.

[26] The Cabinet Secretariat in their Resolution No. 14/1/2/77-CF dated 12 December, 1977, appointed the Committee on Panchayati Raj Institutions. The composition of the Committee was—Shri Asoka Mehta as Chairman and the members included, Shri Karpoori Thakur, Shri Prakash Singh Badal, Shri M.G. Ramachandran, Shri B. Sivaraman, Shri Mangal Deo, Shri Kanwar Mahmood Ali Khan, Shri Annasaheb P. Shinde, Shri E.M.S. Namboodiripad, Shri Siddharaj Dhadda, Prof. Iqbal Narain, Shri Vallabhabhai Patel with S.K.Rau as Member Secretary.

[27] Mathew George, op. cit.

[28] Panchayati Raj: Review and Evaluation, Extract from Reports of various Committees on PRIs- Ashok Mehta Committee-1978, *Kurukshetra,* Vol.XXXVII No.5, February, 1989

[29] ibid p.19.

[30] ibid p.20.

[31] Indira Gandhi National Open University, (1992- Reprint) *Panchayati Raj* in Rural Development- Indian Context , Block -3 on Rural Development Administration. New Delhi.

[32] One of the members of the Committee, Shri Siddharaj Dhadda in his note of dissent on the report of Committee, dated 17 August, 1978, stated, *I am strongly of the opinion that village must be the base, and the Gram Sabha an integral part of Panchayati Raj. Without this base not only Panchayati Raj or democratic decentralization would have no meaning but democracy itself will remain fragile. I am sorry that our Committee has missed a great opportunity of putting democracy on a sure foundation.*

[33] The Govt. of India, constituted a committee in the Planning Commission on 25th March, 1985. The Committee consisted of

Dr G.V.K.Rao as Chairman and members of the committee included Dr P.C.Joshi, Dr B.D. Sharma, Prof. G.Ram Reddy, Dr Asim Dasgupta, Shri Anil C. Shah, Shri K. Subramaniam, Shri J.C. Jetli, Shri G.L. Bailur, Dr V. Venkatesan, Shri B.N. Sahay (for Advisor, Rural Development) and Shivraj Singh as Secretary. Besides these members, Shri M. Subrahmaniam, Shri K. Ramanujam, Shri D. Bandyopadhyay, Dr P.R. Dubhashi, Shri M. Vardarajan, and Dr K.V. Sundaram served as permanent invitees to the committee.

[34] 'Report of the Committee to Review the Existing Administrative Arrangements for Rural Development and Poverty Alleviation Programmes', Department of Rural Development, Ministry of Agriculture, December, 1985.

[36] ibid. p.77-79.

[37] *'Revitalisation of PRIs for democracy and development'*, L.M. Singhvi Committee: 1986 –Extract from Reports on various Committees on PRIs. *Kurukshetra,* February, 1989. p.41.

[39] *Revitalisation of PRIs for democracy and development'*, L.M. Singhvi Committee: 1986 *Kurukshetra,* February, 1989 op. cit p.45.

[40] See op. cit Planning at Grassroots Level (2006).

Photographs	**Sources**
1. Sir Charles Metcalfe	http://en.wikipedia.org/wiki/Charles Metcalfe%2C 1st Baron Metcalfe
2. Lord Rippon	http://www.columbia.edu/itc/mealac/pritchett/00routesdata/1800 1899/britishrule/viceroys/ripon 1.jpg
3. Congress Session-1942	http://www.bbc.bbc.co.uk/ww2peopleswar/timeline/factfiles/images/055 big/jpg
4. Mahatma Gandhi	http://upload.wikimedia.org/wikipedia/scn/1/1d/160px-Maghandi.jpg
5. Pt. Jawahar Lal Nehru	http://www.southasianmedia.net/profile/india/images/nehru 3.jpg
6. Asoka Mehta	http://www.aiimsusa.com/ImageGallery.html (AIIMS Convocation-1966)
7. L. M. Singhvi	http://164.100.24.167/kiosk/whoswho/S27.jpg
8. V. N. Gadgil	http://164.100.24.167/kiosk/whoswho/S27.jpg

3

THE CONSTITUTION (73RD AMENDMENT) ACT, 1992, & THE PROVISIONS OF PANCHAYATS (EXTENSION TO THE SCHEDULED AREAS) ACT, 1996

Pre--Amendment Scenario

Before this amendment, the Panchayati Raj System was not effective the way it should have been. Its powers were limited. The district authorities could dissolve Panchayati Raj Institutions. Elections for these bodies were not regular. Accountability was not a recognised feature of these institutions. The recommendations of the various Committees and Commissions mentioned in Chapter 2 led to the realisation that there was a need to create a strong third tier of governance, which would facilitate the possibility of rural communities influencing their own future. To materialize this, it was considered necessary to give constitutional recognition to this third tier of governance.

Rajiv Gandhi

Undoubtedly, the credit to initiate this process should go to former Prime Minister, late Rajiv Gandhi, who strongly believed in strengthening panchayats by according constitutional status to them. As Bandyopadhyay, rightly comments, "Against this thumb-nail historical sketch of Panchayats in India, it is a bit riddle why and how Rajiv Gandhi—a totally apolitical person to begin with—did realize, appreciate and with single-minded devotion and determination activate an ancient and currently defunct system of governance at the local level—the Panchayat."[1] His first significant statement on Panchayats was made in his inaugural address to the 13th All India Panchayat Parishad Meeting on 22 September, 1986, almost two years after he became the Prime Minister. In this meeting he resolved to strengthen the Panchayati Raj System and said, "If we continue to devise schemes from above, large sections of the population will be left high and dry, and flow of benefits from development will pass over their heads like water on a duck's back for it is not possible for the government agencies to reach each and every individual and to guide him and tell him to do this or that."

Late Rajiv Gandhi's commitment to strengthen Panchayati Raj System got further cemented after he, as the Prime Minister, had a series of workshops with District Collectors, on 'Responsive Administration' between December, 1987 and June, 1988, to understand the problems of rural development in the country. These workshops were held at Bhopal, Hyderabad, Imphal, Jaipur and Coimbatore. The deliberations at the workshops revealed that the District Administration was insensitive to the problems of rural masses and that the funds being provided by the government to bring about rural development was being wasted with gay abandon. At the end of these workshops, it seems that he felt confident that 'the underlying problem was not so much a matter of simplifying procedures or establishing grievances redressal machinery but fundamentally of a systemic nature.'[2] He followed up the outcome of these workshops with a Conference of Chief Ministers. From all these efforts it is clear that his intentions to bring about *Gram Swaraj* through Panchayati Raj were clear and focused. When it was realized that the matter of the Panchayats should be tackled firmly within the

Constitution, the proposals in the shape of the 64th amendment became very important.

The Constitution (73rd Amendment) ACT, 1992[3]

The amendment phase began with the 64th Amendment Bill (1989), which was introduced in Parliament for constituting panchayats in every State at the village, intermediate and district levels. It proposed that the Legislature of a State could by law endow the panchayats with such powers and authority as may be necessary to enable them to function as institutions of self-government. Unfortunately, though the Bill got a two-thirds majority in the Lok Sabha, it was struck down in the Rajya Sabha on October 15, 1989, by just two votes.

The next government headed by V.P. Singh also made an abortive effort to provide Constitutional status to the Panchayati Raj System through the introduction of 74th Amendment. These failures notwithstanding, the Government declared its commitment to the philosophy of ***Power to the People*** and to achieve this objective provided the much needed constitutional status to panchayats. The then Congress-I Government headed by P.V. Narasimha Rao initiated the 73rd Amendment to the Constitution in 1991. A comprehensive amendment was introduced in the form of Constitution (72nd Amendment) Bill in September 1991, which was subsequently referred to a Joint Select Committee of the Parliament in December 1991 for a detailed examination.

V.P. Singh

Finally, after including the necessary amendments, the Amendment was passed with near unanimity in the Lok Sabha on December 22, 1992 and in the Rajya Sabha on December 23, 1992. The Bill got the President's assent on

April 20, 1993 and the Constitution 73rd Amendment Act came into effect from April 24, 1993. This Amendment has, in effect, made the transfer of power to Panchayats a part of the most basic document of this nation—the **Constitution of India.**

The amendment required all the States to amend their respective Panchayat legislations to conform to the Constitution Amendment within one year and to hold elections by April 1995. Those who would delay the process ran the risk of losing assistance from the Central Government, as was announced by the then Prime Minister. All the States complied and adopted new Panchayat legislation by April 23, 1994. A copy of the Constitution (73rd Amendment) Act, 1992 is placed at Annexure-III.

P.V. Narasimha Rao

Special features of the Amendment

a) **Gram Sabha**: Gram Sabha is a body consisting of

Gram Sabha meeting in Pallapalayam, Tamil Nadu

persons registered in the electoral roll of a village or a group of villages which elect a Panchayat. The Act restored the important role of the Gram Sabha. Article 243A states that 'A Gram Sabha may exercise such powers and perform such functions at the village level as the Legislature of a State may, by law, provide.' It is now clear that the primary source of democratic power is a village. A vibrant and enlightened Gram Sabha is central to the success of the Panchayati Raj system. It is also expected that the Gram Sabha will be an active institution for development activities based on local needs.

b) **Three-tier system:** The Act provides for a uniform three-tier system of panchayats (village, intermediate and district level). Only the States with populations less than twenty lakhs are not required to establish a panchayat at the intermediate level.

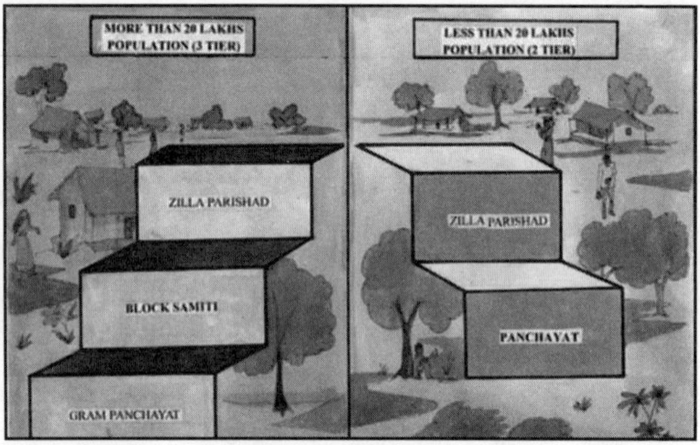

Fig.i Three-tier System

c) **Reservation of Seats:** The Act provides for reservation of seats for Scheduled Castes and Scheduled Tribes in every panchayat in proportion to their population. One-third of seats reserved for Scheduled Castes and Scheduled Tribes are also reserved for women. Not less than one-third of the total number of seats to be filled by direct elections are reserved for women. And such seats are allotted by rotation to different constituencies.

The offices of the chairpersons in the panchayats at the village or any other level are reserved for Scheduled Castes and Scheduled Tribes in proportion to their population. One-third of the total number of offices of chairpersons in the panchayats at each level are also reserved for women.

d) **Composition of Panchayats**: Direct election to the panchayats is one of the distinguishing features of this Amendment. Persons chosen through direct elections from territorial constituencies fill all the seats in a panchayat. The chairperson at the village level is elected in a manner provided by the legislature of the State concerned. The chairpersons at the intermediate and district levels are elected by and from amongst the elected members.

Fig.ii Duration of Panchayats

e) **Duration of Panchayats**: The duration of every panchayat is for a period of five years. If it is dissolved for any reason before the end of this period, elections are held within six months. The reconstituted panchayat functions for the remaining period of the total of five years.

f) **Conduct of elections:** The superintendence, direction and control of the preparation of electoral roll for, and the conduct of, all elections to the panchayats is vested in the State Election Commission. The State Election Commission is also responsible for conducting elections.

g) **Finance Commission:** In order that enough funds are available with the panchayats for initiating various development activities the Constitution (73rd Amendment) Act, 1992, provides for the constitution of a Finance Commission in every State. This Commission was to be constituted by the Governor of each State within one year from the commencement of the Constitution Act, 1992 and subsequently at the end of every five years. The Commission is expected

Fig.iii Development Activities

to be responsible for reviewing financial conditions of panchayats and for making related recommendations to the respective Governors.

h) **Development activities:** The Act gives powers and responsibilities to the panchayats to plan and execute economic development programmes. It involves making plans for economic development, social justice and the implementation of schemes listed in the Eleventh Schedule. The activities earmarked for Panchayat Institutions may be grouped under five categories for academic purposes.

1. *Economic Development*: There are 11 items which talk about economic development. One of them relates to anti-poverty programmes, such as JRY, IRDP, etc. Other areas are agriculture, land improvement, minor irrigation, animal husbandry, fishery, social forestry, minor forest produce, small scale and cottage industry, fuel and fodder.
2. *Education:* There are five items under this category. Primary and Secondary Schools, non-formal education, libraries, technical training, cultural activities, etc.
3. *Health:* There are two items related to health, such as health and sanitation and family welfare.
4. *Welfare, including Women and Child development*: There are four items which include social welfare: welfare of weaker sections, public distribution system, women and child development.
5. *Infrastructure Development*: There are seven items here such as roads, housing, drinking water, markets, electrification, maintenance of community assets, etc.

Among these, there are certain items (apart from the items on anti-poverty programme) which are meant for the poor or the under privileged. Schemes for weaker sections or programmes for women and child development fall under this category. The benefits of public distribution system should also go to the poor. Land reform is central to all, particularly distribution of waste-land enforcement of the tenancy laws constitute a frontal attack on poverty.

District Planning Committee (DPC)

In view of the importance attached to the decentralized planning and to ensure bottom-up-approach, Article 243ZD of part IXA of the Constitution calls for the setting up of a District Planning Committee (DPC) in every district to consolidate the plans prepared by the Panchayats and the Municipalities in the district and to prepare a draft development plan for the district as a whole to be forwarded to the State Planning Department. It has been left to the discretion of the *state legislatures* to make provisions for the composition of the District Planning Committee, including its Chairperson. Since DPC is entrusted with the task of preparing a draft plan for the district as a whole, the proportional representation of elected members from both panchayats and municipal bodies is expected to be ensured.

The Provisions of Panchayats (Extension to the Scheduled Areas) Act, 1996[4]

The Provisions of the Panchayats (Extension to the Scheduled Areas) Act, 1996 (PESA) came into force on 24th December, 1996. This Act extends panchayats to the tribal areas of the ten states namely Andhra Pradesh, Bihar, Jharkhand, Gujarat, Himachal Pradesh, Maharashtra, Madhya Pradesh, Chhatisgarh, Orissa and Rajasthan. It intends to enable tribal societies to assume control over their destiny and to preserve and conserve their traditional rights over natural resources. The State Governments were required to enact their legislations in accordance with the provisions of the Act before the expiry of the one year, i.e., 23rd December, 1997. A copy of the Provisions of the Panchayats (Extension to the Scheduled Areas) Act-1996 is placed at Annexure-IV. The salient features of the Act are:

1. Every village shall have an elected Gram Sabha and it shall be competent to safeguard and preserve the traditions and customs of the people.
2. Gram Sabha shall approve the plans, programmes and projects for social and economic development before their implementation.
3. It would be responsible for the identification or selection of persons as beneficiaries under the poverty alleviation and other programmes.
4. Every Gram Panchayat shall obtain from Gram Sabha a certificate of utilisation of funds for the plans, programmes and projects.
5. The reservation of seats in the Scheduled Areas in every Panchayat shall be in proportion to the population of the communities in the Panchayat.
6. Planning and management of minor water bodies in the Scheduled Areas shall be entrusted to Panchayats at the appropriate level.
7. Recommendations of the Gram Sabha or the Panchayats shall be mandatory for granting of licenses for mining lease for minerals and concessions for the exploitation of minor minerals by auction in the Scheduled Areas.
8. The state legislature shall endow Panchayats and the Gram Sabha specifically with :
   i. power to enforce prohibition or regulate or restrict the sale and consumption of any intoxicants;
   ii. ownership of minor forest produce;
   iii. power to prevent land alienation in the Scheduled Areas;
   iv. power to manage village markets;

v. power to control money lending to Scheduled Tribes' social sectors;
vi. power to control local plans and resources for such plans, including tribal sub-plans; and
vii. the state legislations that may endow Panchayats with powers and authority, as may be necessary, to enable them to function as institutions of self-government, shall contain safeguards to ensure that Panchayats at the higher level do not assume the powers and authority of any Panchayats at the lower level or of the Gram Sabha.

Post Amendment Scenario

The institution of Panchayati Raj, in its rejuvenated form sought to realise the goal of democratic decentralization to accelerate socio-economic development and bring about equity and social justice. The 73rd Amendment Act, 1992 and the subsequent State Legislations were expected to endow Panchayats with such powers and authority, as may be necessary to enable them to function as effective institutions of self-government. Initially there was a positive response from the States, as almost all the States passed their respective State Legislations in conformity with the provisions of the 73rd Amendment and held Panchayat elections. As a result, 2,27,698 panchayats at village level, 5,906 panchayats at intermediate level and 474 panchayats at district level were constituted in the country. About 3.4 million people were elected at these different tiers throughout the country. One could for the first time witness a high degree of uniformity conferred on Panchayats particularly in terms of structure, composition, powers and functions. In the light of the fact that the devolution of functions and authority has not been carried out in letter and spirit, a proper understanding of the post-amendment scenario calls for an in-depth analysis of the 73rd

Amendment itself.

Seventy-Third Amendment—An Analysis

The analysis of the 73rd Amendment reveals that the Panchayati Raj Institutions had to be vested with such authority and power as would enable them to function as effective institutions of self-government. It implies that they have to be democratic in nature (through regular and mandatory elections) with allocated values, priorities and policies necessary to make them effective institutions of self-government. The analysis also reveals that Panchayati Raj Institutions are to act as welfare government, which implies that they have to initiate, plan and executive development activities and bring about social justice. It appears that between the enactment of the 73rd Amendment and the subsequent State Legislations, the necessary amount of thought could not be given to outline the legislative requirements and the related processes that would translate the Amendment into flawless legislation and build for its successful implementation. The whole initial process turned out to be a race for catching the deadline rather than that of realistic thinking. In most cases, some amendments were incorporated in the already existing Acts to make them look ostensibly in conformity with the 73rd Amendment. It seems that the legislatures failed to take cognizance of the profound implications of the constitutional status given to the Panchayats as institutions of Self-Government. Accordingly, Panchayats under the State Acts are institutions that lack the necessary autonomy. There are some State Acts which do not have even the pretension of carving out autonomous jurisdiction for Panchayats. The preambles of these legislations declare that the purpose behind creating Panchayats is to improve rural administration and ensure people's participation in the developmental programmes. Even the Acts of those

States, which, in the statements of their objectives, claim to have created institutions of self-government ultimately end up with creating Panchayat bodies without decentralizing the administrative and financial powers through such bodies.

The most glaring omission in the State Acts relates to the devolution of functions to the panchayats. Even though most State Acts have reproduced in a parrot like manner the 11th Schedule (which lists 29 development activities transferable to panchayats) as it is, few have ear-marked any of the functions/activities of the schedule as the exclusive jurisdiction of the panchayats. Consequently there has been no substantial devolution of administrative and financial powers. In most of the cases, as various studies reveal, the role of panchayats have been reduced to that of agencies of State Government meant to implement various development programmes and schemes. One can very safely and correctly say that panchayats **have not emerged as institutions of Self-Government** as envisaged under the Constitution (73rd Amendment) Act- 1992.

The Institution of Panchayati Raj seeks to realize the goal of decentralized administration and decision-making by people themselves, especially at grass roots level. In an authoritarian form of polity, the local government is necessarily a form of deconcentration, arising out of administrative necessity. On the other hand, in the democratic pattern it assumes the form of decentralization, a politico-administrative mechanism. However, the Indian pattern like the French combines several facets of deconcentration and decentralization, unlike the British and more so, the American form of local government that offers higher degree of decentralization of governance. (Muttalib).[5] This allows us to have a fresh look at the concept of democratic decentralization to be materialized through the Panchayati Raj System. "Experiences with decentralization in developing countries of this region have demonstrated that implementation of pre-determined policies and programmes cannot be taken for granted as a matter of routine and that variety of political, social, economic, behavioural and organizational factors influence the degree to which policies can be implemented."[6]

On the basis of great discussions and debates, which have taken place at various forums, the following are perhaps the basic pre-requisites for materializing the concept of democratic decentralization through the Panchayati Raj system.

- Adequate financial, administrative and technical support to the local organisation;
- Availability of financial assistance/resources;
- Strong local self-government institutions with authority vested in elected representatives of the people;
- Positive attitude of bureaucracy; and
- Effective monitoring and evaluation systems.

Although the Constitution (73rd Amendment) Act- 1992 provides enough scope to ensure the above pre-requisites, it is yet to be seen as to how the PRIs can become real institutions of self-governance.

On the basis of the above analysis, one can safely conclude that the post 73rd Constitution Amendment scenario presents a mixed picture where on the one hand, the necessary devolution of powers and authority has not taken place in letter and spirit, and on the other 34 lakh elected representatives have occupied their positions in the multi-tier set up of the panchayats throughout the country. We also witness successful functioning of some panchayats along side some that are not allowed to function. The process of change has began, but we have to go a long way to realise Gandhiji's dream of "Gram Swaraj" through the Panchayati Raj System in India.

Reference

[1] Bandyopadhyay. D, (2004), *Panchayats and Democracy-Elites versus Dalits in New Issues in Panchayati Raj,* Task Force on Panchayati Raj, Rajiv Gandhi Foundation- Concept Publishing House, New Delhi.

[2] ibid. p 150.

[3] The Constitutional (73rd Amendment) Act, 1992, Ministry of Rural Development, Govt. of India, New Delhi.

[4] The Provisions of the Panchayats (Extension to the Scheduled Areas) Act, 1996 No. 40 of 1996 December, Ministry of Rural Development, Govt. of India, New Delhi.

[5] Multtalib, M.A. "Decentralisation, Local government Institutions and Resource Mobilisation "edited by Hasnat Abdul Hye. BARD, Comilla, 1985.

[6] CIRDAP, 1986, Decentralization policies and programmes: Bangladesh, Indonesia & Nepal.

Photographs	Sources
9. Rajiv Gandhi	http://content.answers.com/main/content/wp/en/thumb/d/dc/140px-Rajiv Gandhi.jpeg
10. V. P. Singh	http://www.thehindu.com/2006/05/02/images/2006050204441001.jpg
11. P. V. Narasimha Roa	http://www.auroville.org/journals&media/avtoday/Jan.2005/narasimha-rao.jpg
12. Gram Sabha Meeting	M.Govarathan. *The Hindu*, Monday, Oct 03, 2005

4

PRINCIPLES OF LOCAL GOVERNANCE

The objectives of local-governance cannot be realized by passing legislations only. The related legislation is necessary, but it is not enough unless its spirit is translated into practice. It is also equally important that both the people in general and the Panchayati Raj functionaries in particular are made aware of the principles of local governance. This will help them to carry out the responsibilities effectively.

At the very outset, it is necessary to remember that we elect representatives for the Legislative Assemblies and the Parliament, from among the electorate of their respective constituencies. Similarly we elect members of the panchayats from among the members of their respective Gram Sabhas. They work as the executive wing of the Gram Sabha. Panchayats are as important at the village level, as Legislative Assemblies at the state level and the Parliament at the national level. They are expected to function both as 'Institutions of Local Self-government' as well as 'Institutions of Development'. The empowerment of Panchayats entails a clear understanding of these two major aspects of their functioning.

Panchayati Raj as a Local Self-Government Institution

The system of rural, local self-government in India is called Panchayati Raj. It is an indigenous concept. Since ancient times, the people in our villages have managed their social and economic affairs on their own. During the British period, Panchayati Raj System passed through various phases. Since then it has come a long way. In order to understand the essence of this major instrument of democratic decentralization, it will be useful to understand and discuss the basic concepts involved in it, namely 'Governance' and 'Local Self-Government'.

Meaning of Governance and Local Self-Government

- ***Meaning of Governance***

In simple words *governance* means the process of decision making together with the process by which these decisions are implemented. Thus governance is a process by which authority in a country is exercised for the common good. It includes:

i) the process by which those in authority are elected or selected, monitored and replaced,
ii) the capacity and the activities of the government to effectively manage its resources and implement sound policies, and
iii) the citizens' and the state's respect for the institutions that govern economic and social interaction among them.

In a democratic set-up, legislature is the body responsible for framing laws for the effective governance of the state. The bureaucracy is to implement these laws honestly so that the state progresses in all respects. In the democratic structure of our country, we have three levels of governance—national or federal, state or regional, and local self-government at grass roots level. Let us now discuss what *local self-government* means.

- ***Meaning of local self-government***

Local self-government implies:[1]

i) a Government run by the local people;
ii) a Government concerned with the local issues;

iii) that the local people can check the activities of the Government; and

iv) that the local people can participate in all the concerns and the functions of the Government.

It advocates increasing accountability and is expected to promote efficiency and improve organizational performances by emphasizing effective management of resources and providing accurate information to take appropriate decisions, and thus leads to greater control of community affairs by the local masses. The Parliament and the State Assemblies cannot be called local self-government, because they are not concerned with the local issues only. Instead they are responsible for bigger areas of activities. Further, the local people do not have any control over the instruments of the State and Central Governments. It is necessary to understand this difference between local self-government and the representative governments at the state and the central level. Let us now discuss Panchayati Raj as an institution of local self-government.

Panchayati Raj as an Institution of Local Self-Government

Panchayati Raj as an institution of local self-government can play an important role in promoting people's participation in the democratic process. It can be instrumental in integrating our traditional wisdom with modernity and in protecting our culture. It can also become an instrument for ensuring social justice. Panchayati Raj can:[2]

- enable rural people plan their own affairs;
- give them a sense of confidence and courage;
- enable people to participate in the democratic process; and
- give equal opportunities of participation to weaker sections of our society.

Panchayati Raj Institutions (PRIs) among other things are also responsible for building schools, dispensaries, *panchayat ghars*, etc., and are likely to get involved in monitoring the functioning of these institutions and their activities. All this may be done by the Gram Panchayat itself, and thus establish its credentials as an effective institution of self-governance. If the Panchayat is successful in ensuring such services to the entire community, especially to the poor people, widows, the handicapped and other needy people, it will become a true expression of self-governance.

Principles of democratic decentralization

Panchayati Raj is an exercise in democratic decentralization, i.e. delegation of power and authority to lower or grass roots levels. The system is based on the following principles:

- There should be a three-tier structure of local self-governing bodies from village to district levels with an organic link among the operations from the lower to the higher levels.
- There should be a genuine devolution of power and responsibility to these bodies.
- Adequate financial resources should be made available to these bodies to enable them discharge their responsibilities appropriately.
- All the development programmes at these levels should be channeled through these bodies.
- The system evolved should be such as to facilitate further decentralization of power and responsibility in the future.

The above principles can be materialized if adequate powers and functions are delegated to the three tiers of Panchayati Raj by the respective State Governments. While as a uniform three-tier structure of local self-government has been put in place through the mandatory provisions of 73rd Constitutional Amendment, the organic linkages among the operations from the lower to the higher levels were expected to be ensured through state intervention. Similarly, devolution of power and responsibilities and the provision of adequate financial resources were left to be decided by the state legislations. Unfortunately, the required interventions and contributions expected of the States have not been coming forth the way they should have. Here there is a lot to be desired.

Panchayati Raj as a Development Institution

Panchayats are also expected to play an important role in planning and implementing various development programmes. They thus assume the role of a development institution. One may recall that after independence India has continually implemented development interventions with the objective of improving the social and economic conditions of the people. One of the major development interventions was the Community Development Programme (CDP) introduced in 1952. The Programme was not a success because of the lack of people's participation in it. It was followed by a series of development interventions, but people's participation continued to be a problem. In the mean time, however, the Central Government continued to introduce various development interventions to catalyse rural development. These, apart from Community Development and allied programmes in the 1950s, included target group approach programmes like Small Farmers Development Agency (SFDA) in the 1970s and employment generation and poverty alleviation programmes like Integrated Rural Development Programme (IRDP), etc. in the 1980s. When all such experiments failed, the policy makers turned towards the Panchayati Raj System in a more deliberate way. Earlier too, from time to time, the importance of the Panchayati Raj System as a mechanism for effective people's participation had got highlighted through the deliberations of various committees like Balvantrai Mehta Committee in 1957, Asoka Mehta Committee in 1977 and so on, but finally these deliberations found their expression in the 73rd Constitutional Amendment in 1993.

Now it is strongly felt that an effective Panchayati Raj System can bring about rapid and integrated development through people's participation. In all the recently re-structured development programmes like SGSY, SGRY, etc. adequate provision has been made for their implementation through the Panchayati Raj Institutions. Thus, the role of Panchayati Raj as a development institution assumes considerable significance. Since we are talking about development, let us first understand the meaning of development.

Meaning of Development

What is development? The moment we talk about development, 'economic growth' comes to our mind immediately. While as economic growth is an important component of development, development goes beyond economic growth to include 'social justice' and 'equitable distribution of the benefits of development' aiming at the overall improvement in the quality of life. Development entails that economic growth has to be supported by (i) institution building and (ii) development mechanisms for re-distribution of benefits. For institution building, Panchayati Raj Institutions become an important mechanism. It can be examined through (i) economic growth and PRIs and (ii) Socio-Political Awareness and Panchayati Raj.

i) Economic Growth and Panchayati Raj Institutions (PRIs)

The Panchayati Raj Institutions can play an important role in bringing about economic prosperity which can be achieved if the following points are kept in mind at the local/panchayat/grass roots level:

- people must be made to understand the problems of their areas, and must be made to find solutions in view of the local resources available to them;
- people should be made to commit themselves to the implementation of development programmes;
- planning must be done at the panchayat level by the people and not thrust upon them by the Government from above;
- people must be encouraged to participate in the programmes meant for their development;
- a high level of transparency should be maintained in the process of undertaking economic activities; and
- people should be given the right to know and question the panchayat representatives about the selection of beneficiaries and the progress of works, the money spent, the kind of labour engaged, etc.

Without observing the above norms, accountability cannot be established and Panchayats cannot be democratic and the rural poor cannot become prosperous or powerful.

ii) Socio-Political Awareness and Panchayati Raj

The concept of development also includes socio-political awareness. People must know their surroundings, their problems, their values, their rights and duties. Without awareness about these basics, their development is incomplete. Panchayati Raj Institutions can use a forum like Gram Sabha to create awareness among their members about the local problems and the important concerns pertaining to development such as the need for education, health, sanitation, family planning, nutrition, etc. Periodic and regular elections to panchayats on non-party basis will inculcate in them the lessons of operating democracy at grass roots.

Role of Panchayati Raj Institutions in the Planning and Implementation of Anti-poverty Programmes

It is an admitted fact that panchayats constitute the local governments of the people. A democratic government is one that involves people to take decisions about the activities that directly concern their locality and lives. Naturally, panchayats should allow and help the rural poor to participate in the developmental activities directly. For example, if a Gram Panchayat decides to build a school, dispensary or drainage system, the people who need these facilities should decide what kind of the school, dispensary or drainage system they need. Panchayats should not keep people at a distance. No work or decision should be kept as a secret.

Anti-poverty programmes should not be seen as charities. They are mechanisms meant to give back those rights to the poor people which have been denied to them by the rich and the powerful. The poor have the right to decide what their needs are and what plans and programmes they must use. Anti-poverty programmes should be planned at the local level, i.e. at the Gram Panchayat level. Why? A panchayat is in a position to identify the poor, because they know everyone in the village. It is necessary that open meetings are held where all the people can meet and discuss the village problems and also anti-poverty programmes. It is the duty of the elected members of panchayats to hold regular Gram Sabha meetings. These meetings will be immensely useful, if the following norms are kept in mind and followed sincerely:

- explain anti-poverty and other schemes to the people very clearly in the language that they understand;
- encourage the poor people to speak in these meetings; (Many people may be hesitant to give their views in a meeting for many reasons. The elected members should create an atmosphere that enables the people to speak without fear.)
- try to understand their views and thoughts; and
- identify the people who are really poor.

There are a number of anti-poverty programmes under implementation in various States. In the changing scenario, panchayats are expected to play an important role in the planning and implementation of these programmes. As it is not possible to cover all the development programmes being or expected to be implemented by the Panchayati Raj Institutions, the discussion here will be confined to the role of Panchayats in implementing some major centrally sponsored anti-poverty programmes.

Current Strategy: Main poverty alleviation schemes

Under the current strategy, the main poverty alleviation schemes, in which Panchayats also are expected to play an important role, include the following:

- **Self-Employment (Credit/Subsidy) Programme,** earlier consisting of six schemes, has been revamped and merged into one programme called the **Swarnajayanti Gram Swarozgar Yojana (SGSY).**
- **Wage Employment Programme,** earlier consisting of two schemes, namely Jawahar Rozgar Yojana (JRY) (later renamed Jawahar Gram Samridhi Yojana and Employment Assurance Scheme (EAS), has been revamped and merged into one

programme named the **Sampoorn Gramin Rozgar Yojana (SGRY).**
- **Rural Housing Programme**, consists mainly of **Indira Awaas Yojana (IAY).**

Now we will briefly discuss each one of them:

i) Swarnajayanti Gram Swarozgar Yojana (SGSY)[3]

There were a number of schemes being implemented under the self-employment category of the poverty alleviation programmes. These were viewed as separate programmes in themselves. This resulted in a lack of inter-programme interaction and absence of the much needed links among these programmes. Their implementation got concerned more about achieving individual programme targets rather than focusing on any substantive means of sustainable income generation. To rectify this situation, the Government of India revamped the self-employment programmes and a new programme known as the **Swarnajayanti Gram Swarozgar Yojana (SGSY)** was launched in April, 1999. This is a holistic programme covering all aspects of self-employment like organization of the poor into self-help groups, training, credit, technology, infrastructure and marketing. The earlier programmes like IRDP, TRYSEM, DWCRA, SITRA, MWS and GKY are no longer in operation now.

Objectives

The objective of the Swarnajayanti Gram Swarozgar Yojana (SGSY) is to provide sustainable income to the rural poor. The programme aims at setting up a large number of micro-enterprises in the rural areas. The basic idea is that the rural poor in India have varied competencies and if they are provided with necessary support at the right time, they can become very successful producers of valuable goods and services.

SGSY is basically a holistic programme of micro-enterprises covering all the necessary aspects of self-employment which include the following:

- Organization of the rural poor into self-help groups
- Their capacity building
- Planning of activity clusters
- Infrastructure build-up
- Technology
- Credit and Marketing

Who can benefit from SGSY?

Under the Scheme of SGSY the beneficiaries are known as *Swarozgaris. Swarozgaris* can be either individuals or a group of individuals. It is important to remember that SGSY emphasizes the group approach. Whether it is an individual or a group, the beneficiaries or *Swarozgaris* are selected from the list of the below poverty line (BPL) households, which is duly approved by the Gram Sabha. The SGSY focuses particularly on disadvantaged groups among the rural poor. Accordingly, at least 50 per cent of the *Swarozgaris* are expected to be Scheduled Castes and Scheduled Tribes, 40 per cent women and 3 per cent the disabled among the rural poor.

The guidelines have been just revised (December, 2006) to give special attention to minorities living below the poverty line. In the guidelines under, 'Safeguards for Weaker Sections', word 'Minorities' have been added. The State Governments have to now ensure that the percentage of BPL families from the minority communities on the list of beneficiaries of SGSY is proportionate to their population in the respective states. Minorities include Muslims, Sikhs, Christians, Buddhists, Parses and others notified in the National Commission for Minorities Act, 1992. But in States where these communities are in the majority, they do not qualify as a 'minority'.

Selection of Beneficiaries

There are two types of beneficiaries to be selected under SGSY—individual beneficiaries or *Swarozgaris* and Self-Help Groups. The process of the selection of individual *Swarozgaris* begins as soon as the Block SGSY Committee finalizes the list of the selected villages every year, about which the Sarpanches concerned are duly informed. The individual Swarozgaris are normally selected in the Gram Sabha. However, at times, a Gram Sabha held at Panchayat headquarters may not benefit from the participation of all the BPL families. In order to ensure maximum participation, a 3-member team consisting of the BDO or his/her representative, the Banker concerned and the Sarpanch is expected to visit each household in the Panchayat area. This visit has to be taken up as per a schedule which should be duly publicized. The team identifies the persons who can be covered under the designated key activities from among the BPL families. The process of identification has to be completed carefully so as to ensure that the really needy ones are selected as the beneficiaries.

The other category of beneficiaries comprises Self-Help Groups. These are based on the organization of the rural poor through the process of social mobilization. This process of social mobilization enables them to form their own organizations (self-help groups) in which they can participate fully and directly and take decisions on all the issues related to poverty eradication. Now let us discuss in detail as to what these Self-Help Groups are.

What is a Self-Help Group (SHG)?

A Self-Help Group (SHG) is an organization of the poor people at grass roots level formed to exploit their potential for their own betterment. It emerges as a result of the process of social mobilization, which enables them to build their own organizations (Self-Help Groups) for the eradication of poverty. They then effectively participate in these groups and take decisions on all issues (concerning poverty and its eradication) which affect their lives. These groups have the advantage of receiving assistance either in terms of credit and technology or market guidance.

A SGSY group may have 10-20 members. The minimum number may be even five for minor irrigation projects or when members are disabled persons. The group should not include more than one member from the same family and no one should be a member of more than one group. One can say that a group has been formed, when the group is able to:

i) meet regularly (weekly or fortnightly);
ii) function in a democratic manner by allowing free exchange of views;
iii) participate in the decision making process;
iv) draw up an agenda for each meeting and take up discussion according to the agenda;
v) follow common rules and procedures for working together;
vi) build its corpus of funds through regular savings and use it to advance loans to the members; and
vi) maintain simple basic records and operate a group account.

In forming Self-Help Groups under the SGSY, it should be noted that 50 per cent of the groups formed in each block should be exclusively for women. Regarding disabled persons, wherever possible, the groups formed should be around a particular disability. If that is not possible, then the people suffering from various disabilities could be combined to form a Self-Help Group of disabled persons.

Grading of SGSY Self-Help Groups

We have explained above as to how SHGs are formed

under the SGSY. It is important to put every SHG so formed to a test to know how far it has evolved into a good group and whether it is ready to move on to the next stage. This is done through a *grading exercise.* This takes place after six months of the formation of SHGs. The objective of the grading exercise is to identify the weaknesses (if any) of a group, and to help the group to overcome them, and thus, develop into a sound group. During the grading exercise the primary focus is on weak groups and all efforts are made by the DRDAs to rectify the weaknesses of such groups. A Self-Help Group passes through two types of gradation. The first grading begins when a group completes six months in operation. It is necessary to ascertain whether the group has remained viable and sound during this period. It can only then enter the first grade of the second stage and receive the Revolving Fund and take up capacity building (training) of its members.

Six months after receiving the Revolving Fund, the Self-Help Group reaches the second stage of grading. At this stage the basic objective of grading is to find out whether the Self-Help Group is capable of taking an economic activity through higher levels of investment.

Role of the Block SGSY Committee

The Block SGSY Committee has a very important role to play in the process of identifying the key activities. In rural areas some poor families do possess some assets such as land etc. Efforts should be directed in ways so that those who have small pieces of land are enabled to cross the poverty line by making additional investments on their land, such as sinking of wells or other irrigation facilities, pump sets, etc. The next category of the rural poor is that of the people who possess some skills. They may be primarily the rural artisans who form a large segment of the rural society. The programme envisages covering the rural artisans to a significant extent. Another category is the unemployed educated youth who would have been trained under the TRYSEM. An inventory of such people may be made to find out which activities are best suited to their training for the development of the area concerned. The Block SGSY Committee can identify activities after consulting the following groups of people/ institutions:

- NABARD or other Banks of the area;
- Industrial/technical organisations;
- Local Khadi and Village Industries Officials;
- District Manager of District Industries Centre;
- As many Sarpanches as possible in the block; and
- Groups of the rural poor such as the landless labour, the educated unemployed, those rural poor having land, the rural artisan groups, etc.

Based on the above consultation process, the Block SGSY Committee must identify about 8-10 activities. These activities may be ranked in the order of preference. This list should then be placed before the general body of the Panchayat Samiti (Block Panchayat) for their recommendations or comments. Then, the list of selected key activities, along with the recommendations or comments of the Panchayat Samiti must be forwarded by the BDO to the District SGSY Committee for onward transmission to the Assistant Commissioner Development.

Marketing the goods produced by the Swarozgaris is an important task under the SGSY. If there is a proper market for the sale of their products, the Swarozgaris will not lose interest in the programme and it will continue, and thus become sustainable. The PRIs can play an important role both in facilitating the marketing of goods so produced by these Self-Help Groups as well as in sustaining these activities in their respective areas.

ii) Sampoorn Grameen Rozgar Yojana (SGRY)[4]

All the economic activities in villages are closely related to seasons. You must have experienced this phenomenon in your own village as well. During certain seasons, there is enough demand for labour. At certain other times, there is little demand for labour. As a result, the rural poor and landless labourers do not get regular paid-work throughout the year. Most of the time, they remain unemployed or under-employed. Development intervention through the introduction of wage employment schemes has been found to be the most effective strategy for the alleviation of poverty, reduction of inequalities as well as improvements in the nutritional intake of the poor. This, in turn, is expected to be instrumental in maintaining a relatively high rate of economic growth. With this in view, a number of wage-employment schemes have been introduced from time to time to facilitate faster growth in the rural areas and to increase the opportunities of employment by gradually engineering the market oriented economy in the rural areas of the country.

Background

During the first four years of the Seventh Five Year Plan period, there were two wage-employment programmes in existence, namely the National Rural Employment Programme (NREP) and the Rural Landless Employment Guarantee Programme (RLEGP). These programmes were merged into a single programme called the Jawahar Rozgar Yojana (JRY) in April 1989. The strategy for the implementation of JRY was modified in 1993-94 and then it was carried out through three streams. The first stream consisting of general works and two sub-schemes, namely, Indira Awaas Yojana, and Million Wells Scheme. The second stream, which was called intensified JRY was being implemented in 120 identified backward districts.

The third stream consisted of special and innovative projects.

After evaluating the outcome of JRY, it was felt that there was a need to develop village infrastructure based on local needs. Accordingly, the Government decided to streamline and restructure Jawahar Rozgar Yojana with its new focus on the development of rural infrastructure and it was renamed Jawahar Gram Samridhi Yojana on 1st April 1999.

While the Jawahar Gram Samridhi Yojana (JGSY) was a rural infrastructure development scheme, the Employment Assurance Scheme (EAS) was the only additional wage-employment scheme for rural areas introduced in 1993. And, to give focused attention to improvements in wage-employment, infrastructural development and food security in the rural areas, the Ministry of Rural Development reviewed these schemes. Based on the outcome of the review, it was decided to merge EAS with JGSY and to launch a new scheme, which was launched in September 2001 under the name the Sampoorna Grameen Rozgar Yojana (SGRY).

Objectives of the SGRY

The SGRY has two fold objectives:

1. the primary objective is to provide additional and supplementary wage-employment in all rural areas and thereby provide food security and improve nutritional intake among the rural poor; and
2. to create durable community, social and economic assets and effect infrastructural development in rural areas in the long-term.

Beneficiaries under the SGRY

All the rural poor, particularly those who are in need of wage-employment and also desire to do manual and unskilled work in and around their village or habitat, are entitled for benefits under the SGRY. The SGRY, however, provides special safeguards for the weaker sections and women.

Implementation

The SGRY is implemented at two levels. At the first level activities are implemented by the District and Intermediate/Block Panchayat and at the second by the Gram Panchayat. Here we will discuss works to be taken up at the Gram Panchayat level.

Tasks to be undertaken at the Village/Gram Panchayat Level

Emphasis is on the creation of durable, productive community assets. Therefore, priority is to be given to the following tasks:

i) Infrastructural support for the SGSY.
ii) Infrastructure required for supporting agricultural activities in the Village Panchayat areas.
iii) Community infrastructure for education, health as well as internal and link roads.
iv) Desilting and renovation of traditional village tanks/ponds.

At the village/Gram panchayat level, emphasis is not only on the purely material oriented works but also on the labour intensive works. It has to be kept in mind that the works taken up must be sustainable and cost effective.

Allocation of Resources

The SGRY is a Centrally Sponsored Scheme and the cash component of the cost of the whole programme is shared by the Centre and the States in the ratio of 75:25 but the Centre provides 100% funds for the programmes implemented in the Union Territories. Of the total resources allocated under the SGRY, 50% is earmarked for distribution among Village/Gram Panchayats for the generation of supplementary wage employment and the creation of demand driven community/village infrastructure, which includes durable assets to enable the rural poor to increase opportunities for sustained employment. Under the SGRY, Central Assistance is released directly to the DRDAs and Zilla Parishads, and the State Governments also release their corresponding shares to the DRDAs and ZPs. In turn the funds are disbursed to the Block Panchayats and the Village/Gram Panchayats by the DRDAs/ZPs. The DRDAs/ZPs have to release the funds and the foodgrains to the Panchayat/Block Samitis and Village/Gram Panchayats concerned within 15 days of their receipt from the Central/State Governments as the case may be.

Funds available from other sources like market committees, cooperatives, NGOs, NRIs and other institutions may also be dovetailed with the SGRY funds for similar purposes.

Planning of the SGRY

The whole SGRY programme is based on the formulation and implementation of an Annual Action Plan. Accordingly, no work is taken up unless it forms part of the Annual Action Plan. The works included in the Annual Action Plan are based essentially on the needs of the individuals and the community concerned. For both the cases, i.e. individual employment as well as the community infrastructural development, works are carefully prioritized. Taking into account the availability of resources and the priorities of works, it is advisable and essential that emphasis is given to those works that can be completed normally within one year and in extraordinary situations within two years. It is necessary that the following points are carefully noted:

- Before the beginning of each financial year, every Zilla Parishad/DRDA, Panchayat/Block Samiti and Village/Gram Panchayat prepares an Annual Action Plan. While preparing the Annual Action Plan first priority is given to the completion of the incomplete works, if any.
- The Annual Action Plan prepared by the Village/Gram Panchayat is fully discussed and also finally approved in the meetings of the Gram Sabha.
- The approved Annual Action Plan is then intimated to the Block Samiti and Zilla Parishad/District Rural Development Agency.

Execution of Works

The entire work pertaining to co-ordination, supervision, reviewing and monitoring of the works under the SGRY is the responsibility of the Village/Gram Panchayats, which actually execute them. In fact, the Panchayats have the power to execute works/schemes up to Rs. 1,00,000/- with the approval of the Gram Sabha. No other administrative and/or technical approval is necessary for such works.

iii) Indira Awaas Yojana (IAY)[5]

Shelter is one of the basic human requirements and it needs to be met on priority basis. For a common person, owning a house not only provides economic security but also helps in protecting one's family from the harsh summer/moonsoon. It also brings about a social change and stability through which a person can integrate easily and properly with the immediate social environment. Although a number of initiatives have been taken from time to time to provide adequate housing to the rural poor, it was only during the 1980s that special attention was paid to the construction of houses in rural areas particularly for those belonging to Scheduled Castes/Tribes and the freed bonded labourers. A scheme called the Indira Awaas Yojana (IAY) for providing housing facilities to the rural poor was launched during 1985-86 as a sub-scheme of the Rural Landless Employment Guarantee Programme (RLEGP), which later on in April 1989 became a part of the Jawahar Rozgar Yojana (JRY). However, the Indira Awaas Yojana (IAY) was made an independent scheme with effect from January, 1996.

Objectives of the IAY

The main objective of the Indira Awaas Yojana is to provide help in the construction/up-grading of dwelling units for/of the members of Scheduled Castes/Tribes, freed bonded labourers in rural areas and also the rural poor (not belonging to Scheduled Castes/Tribes) living below the poverty line by providing them with a lump sum financial assistance.

Target Beneficiaries of the IAY

The main target groups of the Indira Awaas Yojana (IAY) till 1992-93 were the members of the Scheduled Castes, Scheduled Tribes and the freed bonded labourers living below the poverty line in rural areas. Its scope was extended in 1993-94 to cover the non-Scheduled Caste/Tribe rural poor, subject to the condition that the benefits to the non-SC/ST rural poor do not exceed 40% of the total allocation. In 1995-96, its scope was further extended to cover the families of the servicemen of the armed and paramilitary forces killed in action irrespective of the income criterion subject to the condition that they should:

- be residing in rural areas;
- be houseless or in need of upgrading their shelters; and
- not be covered by any other housing scheme.

Further, benefits have also been extended to ex-servicemen and retired members of the paramilitary forces so long as they fulfil the normal eligibility conditions of the Indira Awaas Yojana. Three per cent (3%) of the funds are reserved for the benefit of the physically and mentally challenged (disabled) persons living below the poverty line in rural areas.

The Process of Identifying Beneficiaries

The process of identifying beneficiaries under the IAY as per the guidelines issued by the Ministry of Rural Development, Government of India, involves the following steps:

- The District Rural Development Agency (DRDA)/ District Level Panchayat is expected to decide the number of houses to be constructed/upgraded under the IAY scheme panchayat-wise for the district concerned during a particular financial year.
- The above decision is to be conveyed to the Gram Panchayats.
- The Gram Panchayats are expected to hold Gram Sabha meetings and select beneficiaries for the IAY according to the guidelines and the target allotted to them.
- The Gram Panchayat is expected to keep the Panchayat Samiti informed by sending a list of the selected beneficiaries to them.

The priorities in selecting beneficiaries under the IAY scheme are detailed below:

i) The first priority goes to freed bonded labourers.
ii) The second priority goes to SC/ST households. Among the SC/ST households, the sub-priorities are those SC/ST households that are victims of

atrocities; SC/ST households which are headed by widows and/or unmarried women; SC/ST households affected by flood, fire, earthquake, cyclone and/or similar natural calamities; and then the other SC/ST households.

iii) The families/widows of the personnel (from defence services/paramilitary forces) killed in action receive the third priority.

iv) The fourth priority in the selection of beneficiaries goes to non-SC/ST households living below the poverty line.

v) The next in the priority list come the physically and mentally challenged persons living below the poverty line. Three per cent (3%) of the funds out of the total allocation have been earmarked for this group.

vi) The sixth priority goes to ex-servicemen and retired persons of the paramilitary forces.

vii) The last priority will involve those who have been displaced on account of developmental projects and nomadic, semi-nomadic and de-notified tribals.

Special attention needs to be given to the following conditions:

In the selection and allotment of the IAY houses, it is very important to remember that:

- The selection of the beneficiaries is subject to the condition that the households of all the above categories except (iii) are Below Poverty Line (BPL).
- The allotment of house is in the name of the female member of the beneficiary household. Alternatively, the house is to be allotted jointly in the names of the husband and the wife.

Allocation and distribution of funds

It is a fact that the price levels increase from time to time.

Taking this into account the cost norms under the IAY have undergone changes from time to time. The expenditure allowed for a house under the IAY at present is as follows:

Table-1
Unit cost for Construction and Upgrading

Items	Plain Areas	Hilly/Difficult Areas
Construction of a house with a sanitary latrine and a smokeless chula (oven)	Rs. 25,000/-	Rs. 27,500/-
Upgrading an un-serviceable house	Rs. 12,500	Rs. 12,500/-

Source: Guidelines for IAY (Effective from 1-4-2004), Ministry of Rural Development, GOI.

Sanitary latrines and smokeless *chulhas* are to be provided with each IAY house. A latrine may be constructed away from the IAY house on the site of the beneficiary. Wherever possible, efforts should be made to dovetail funds from the Total Sanitation Campaign (TSC) for providing sanitary latrines so that more money may be made available for the construction of the IAY houses. In case, the beneficiary is unable to construct a sanitary latrine due to one or the other reason, an amount of Rs. 600/- will have to be deducted from the assistance provided for the construction of the new IAY house or for upgrading an unserviceable *kutcha* house. Similarly, where smokeless *chulha* is not possible, a deduction of Rs.100/- will have to be made from the assistance provided. However, it is always in the interests of the IAY beneficiary to avail him/herself of both the smokeless *chulha* and the sanitary latrine provisions.

Ban on Contractors or Departmental Construction

It is very important to remember that no contractor is now allowed for the construction of the IAY houses. If any case of construction through a contractor comes to the notice of the authorities concerned, the Government of India reserves the right to recover the releases made to the State for the IAY houses concerned. Nor should any houses be constructed by any Government Department. Government departments or organizations can, however, give technical assistance or arrange for coordinated supply of raw materials. The spirit of the IAY is that the IAY houses are not to be constructed and delivered by any external agency. On the other hand, they are to be constructed by the beneficiaries themselves. They can, however, engage labour if necessary.

Involvement of Voluntary Organisations

As mentioned above, the beneficiaries need to be motivated to use sanitary latrines and smokeless *chulhas*. Local voluntary agencies that have a good record of work can be associated with the construction of IAY houses. Even supervision, guidance and monitoring of construction can be entrusted to these non-governmental organizations. In particular, their help can be taken in motivating and popularizing the use of sanitary latrines and smokeless *chulhas*.

Inventory of Houses

In order to have a proper record, the implementing agency is supposed to have a complete list/inventory of houses constructed under the IAY. Gram Panchayats are better placed for this task and it is desirable that they also maintain records of the houses allotted and constructed under the IAY under their jurisdictions. Such records should include the following details:

- Date of the start and the completion of the construction of the house;
- Name of the village and block in which the house is located; and
- The name, address, occupation and category of the beneficiary concerned and other relevant information.

Transparency in the Implementation of the IAY

You will agree that transparency plays an important role in checking wrong utilization of funds and other irregularities. Lack of transparency is the root-cause of many problems and complaints related to works taken up under this programme. People have the right to have access to the information which affects their lives. Keeping this in view, the IAY provides disclosure of the necessary information at various levels viz. the village, the block and the district levels. The type of information expected to be available for the public at the village/Gram Panchayat level may, among other things, include the following:

- List of the people below the poverty line;
- List of the disaster resistant construction features suitable for the region/locality;
- List of the beneficiaries during the preceding and the current years;
- Funds allocated for the IAY for the village concerned;
- IAY guidelines/criteria for selecting the beneficiaries; and
- IAY/GOI *sign boards* displayed on the allotted houses.

New Initiative and Future Strategy

The Government is attaching a lot of importance to the IAY. The Ministry of Rural Development has conducted a number of workshops on rural housing, which were attended by people's representatives, Panchayati Raj functionaries, NGOs and technical and administrative personnel of the State Governments. There is a felt need for standardizing, popularizing and replicating cost-effective, disaster resistant and environment-friendly house construction technologies, designs and materials and also developing ideal and sustainable rural human settlements consistent with the geo-climatic variations and the natural disaster proneness of the locations concerned. It has been decided to improve the quality of houses constructed under the IAY by disseminating relevant information developed by various agencies on all these aspects. DRDAs are expected to take full advantage of the findings and recommendations of these workshops and seminars. Similarly, Gram Panchayats should attempt to procure information about these new initiatives so as to disseminate it among the potential and the existing beneficiaries of the IAY scheme.

We have briefly discussed above some essential features of three important rural development interventions, namely the SGSY, the SGRY and the IAY. Our discussion has been limited to those aspects of the guidelines which are relevant at the Gram Panchayat level. There are many other aspects of the guidelines which have not been covered here, mainly because they are not directly related to Gram Panchayat operations.

References

[1] Panchayat—Institutions of Self-Governance (2001), Block-1 Unit-4 of the self-learning print material prepared under Panchayati Raj Project, IGNOU, New Delhi.

[2] ibid p. 9.

[3] Government of India, 1999, *Swarnjayanti Gram Swarozgar Yojana: Guidelines,* Ministry of Rural Development, New Delhi and Government of India, 2003-2004, *Annual Report,* Ministry of Rural

Development, New Delhi.

[4] Aslam, M. 2003, *Wage Employment Programmes,* Panchayati Raj Project, IGNOU, New Delhi and Government of India, 2004, *Guidelines, Sampoorna Grameen Rozgar Yojana (SGRY),* Ministry of Rural Development, New Delhi.

[5] Government of India, 2000, *Rural Housing Schemes-Guidelines,* National Mission for Rural Housing and Habitat, Ministry of Rural Development, New Delhi.

5

EMPOWERMENT OF PANCHAYATS—A PERSPECTIVE

What does the term, 'empowerment' imply here? Essentially it is *an enabling process to make people capable of taking decisions concerning their development and for changing their lives for better.* The Panchayati Raj Institutions (PRIs), through 73rd Constitutional Amendment, have been ordained to empower the people at three appropriate levels. The Amendment provided institutional mechanism and was meant to rekindle the flame of self-governance. The basic question arises as to what was the basic spirit behind this legislation? Was it limited to the passing of Conformity Acts and endowing panchayats with some administrative and financial powers or to make them genuine institutions for participatory self-government. The emphasis over the last about one and a half decade has been on the former, which has made panchayats mere implementing agencies of pre-conceived schemes passed on to them, with funds, as Centrally or State sponsored schemes. This was not the basic spirit behind this historic legislation. The basic objective of the democratic decentralization through reactivation of the Panchayati Raj system was to realise Gandhiji's concept of ***Gram Swaraj***. This objective has not been achieved. There are a number of factors which need to be addressed to materialize the concept of empowerment. These can be grouped as follows:

Gram Sabha

The success of Panchayati Raj System in India is not possible unless adequate powers are vested in the Gram Sabha, which has to serve as the **heart and soul of the Panchayati Raj System.** It is the only forum, which can give expression to the collective wisdom, aspirations and the will of the people. Gram Sabha could not be turned into the effective body, which would have given expression to the collective wisdom, aspiration and the will of the people. The experience suggests that there is a lack of adequate participation in the Gram Sabha meetings and at places the rural elite hijack these meetings. In some other cases, the Gram Sabha is turned into a discussion forum only.

Fig. iv Gram Sabha

A review of the State Acts reveals that most of the State Legislatures failed to take cognizance of the profound implications of the constitutional status given to the Panchayats as institutions of self-government. Accordingly, the panchayats under most of the State Acts, are ***institutions that lack autonomy.*** There are some State Acts which do not even pretend to carve out any autonomous jurisdiction for Panchayats. The preambles of these legislations declare that the purpose behind creating

Panchayats is to improve rural administration and ensure participation of the people in the developmental programmes rather than materializing the concept of self-governance. Even the Acts of those States, which proclaim to create institutions of self-government in the statements of objectives, end up ultimately creating panchayat bodies without decentralizing the administrative and financial powers through such bodies and without vesting the necessary authority in the ***Gram Sabha to function as a vibrant and dynamic institution.***

The most glaring omission in the State Acts is one relating to the devolution of powers to the Panchayats and, equally important omission relating to the powers and functions to be provided for Gram Sabha. The Article 243-A of the Constitution expected State Legislatures to provide the Gram Sabha with such powers and to charge it to perform such functions at the village level as would help in materializing the concept of democratic decentralizing. In practice, the State Legislatures have not given any thought to this vital aspect and a majority of them expect the Gram Sabha to discuss:

- annual statement of accounts and audit the report;
- administrative report of the preceding year;
- proposal of fresh taxation and enhancement of existing taxes; and
- selection of schemes, beneficiaries and locations.

If one looks more closely into the State Acts, one finds that the State Acts have not been able to add anything new to the functions of the Gram Sabha. For example, if we look at the Andhra Pradesh Panchayati Raj Act, 1994, it becomes clear from the comparative analysis of the past and the present Acts that, except for the selection of schemes/beneficiaries and locations, all other matters to be considered by the Gram Sabha are the same as provided in the Andhra Pradesh Gram Panchayat Act, 1964.

There are more or less similar provisions provided in all the State Acts for formation of the Gram Sabha, membership of Gram Sabha, meetings of the Gram Sabha and the quorum. There are some variations in the processes as far as convening of the Gram Sabha is concerned. In cases like Andhra Pradesh, it is to be convened by an executive officer. In the case of Madhya Pradesh, by a secretary and in other cases by the Sarpanch. In some State Acts, like those of Bihar, Goa, Manipur and Tripura, there is a mention about the Gram Sabha forming one or more vigilance committees consisting of persons who are not members of the Gram Panchayat. These committees are expected to supervise the work of the Gram Panchayat. The review of the role and responsibilities of the Gram Sabha in the State Panchayat Acts reveals that in most of the cases, its role is largely advisory. Similarly, a provision mentioned in most of the State Acts is that the Panchayat shall give due consideration to the recommendations of the Gram Sabha. It clearly implies that the Gram Sabha is a recommending body and that the decision-making authority vests in the Gram Panchayat. In order to materialize the concept of 'Empowerment of Panchayats', it is necessary that adequate provisions are made through amendments so that approving and sanctioning powers as well as monitoring functions are vested in the Gram Sabha to allow Panchayats to become vibrant and dynamic institutions.

Devolution of Powers and Functions

The Article 243 (G) of the Constitution stipulates endowment by law and by the legislature of a State of, such powers and authorities on Panchayats 'as may be necessary to enable them to function as institutions of Self-Government'. The second Para of 243 (G) adds 'and such a law may contain provisions for the devolution of powers and responsibilities' upon Panchayats at the appropriate level subject to such conditions as may be specified therein in respect of (i) preparation of plans for economic development and social justice and, (ii) planning and implementation of schemes for economic development and social justice as may be entrusted to them including those in relation to the matters listed in the 11th Schedule.

The Article 243 G of the Constitution visualises PRIs as institutions of self government but simultaneously it leaves the *extent of devolution of powers and functions* to the will of the State Legislatures. It therefore becomes apparent that unless this crucial will of the State Government concerned is exercised, these bodies can not assume their new role as institutions of self governance, mainly for social and economic development of their respective areas. In fact due to these lacunae left in the 73rd Constitutional Amendment (of leaving Schedule 11 at the discretion of the State Governments), only a few States have given partial functional and financial autonomy to these institutions.

Activity Mapping

The experiences show that the most glaring omissions in the State Acts as stated above is one relating to the devolution of functions to the Panchayats. Even though most State Acts have reproduced in a parrot-like manner the 11th Schedule, few have earmarked any of the functions/ activities of the Schedule as exclusive jurisdiction of a particular tier of the Panchayat. It is noticed that powers and functions have been assigned to PRIs without keeping any cardinal principle in mind. There is overlapping of areas, functions and responsibilities amongst the government agencies in general, and the three levels of PRIs in particular. There is no clear-cut mapping of the functions or activities at different tiers of panchayats.

What has been indicated above requires rationalization of the activities to be entrusted to Panchayats, i.e. we need to revisit the 11th Schedule and see how many and which of the activities listed there can realistically be assigned to Panchayats for implementation. In this connection I must quote what Shri Mani Shankar Aiyer, who aptly explained what 'Activity Mapping' is all about. He said,[1] "But how do you prepare a plan, unless you know what your jurisdiction is and what resources are available with you. To determine the resources you ought to know what functions are expected from you. This requires what we call (many people have difficulty in understanding the term—may be we have to use a better expression) 'activity mapping', which is based on the principle (of working on clearly demarcated responsibility/function areas). For example, there are five types of roads in India. The *national highways* are the responsibility of the Centre and the *state highways* are the responsibility of State Governments. Of the three other types of roads—the major district roads should certainly be the responsibility of the major districts of the states; other district roads (ODRs) will be the responsibility of intermediary panchayats and village roads and village link roads, in my opinion, should go to village panchayats. Here, you have a clear division of work as there is no overlapping. Moreover, the principle of subsidiarity is built into it. It is evident to me that a village road is built by a village panchayat, but an ODR cannot be looked after by one panchayat alone, because it crosses the jurisdiction of several panchayats and similarly a major district road is a road which serves the entire district. You can not have a smaller body looking after a district road for the simple reason that no panchayat can look after a state highway and no state can look after a national highway."

It is a general feeling that the role of Panchayats in all cases has been reduced to that of agencies of the State

Governments. Empowerment of panchayats will remain a distant dream without effective and clear-cut devolution of functions through 'Activity Mapping'. With consistent persuasion of the Ministry of Panchayati Raj through round tables and other forums including meetings of the Committee of Secretaries, some States are undertaking 'Activity Mapping' or reviewing existing Activity Maps with a view to carrying forward the process of effective devolution of functions. The status of 'Activity Mapping ' as provided in the mid-term review of Panchayati Raj presents a mixed picture. It notes:[2] "The Kerala, Karnataka and West Bengal have completed activity mapping, as envisaged in the 73rd Amendment. Sikkim has released a very thorough Activity Map and Punjab is on the verge of doing so. Haryana and Orissa have implemented activity mapping in respect of a limited number of matters but have, admittedly, not yet issued the requisite notifications for financial devolution in accordance with activity mapping. Maharashtra and Gujarat are States with a long history of devolution of powers to Panchayats and they claim that they have delineated the functions clearly in the Panchayati Raj legislation itself. They are joined by Goa, which has detailed provisions in the law that spell out the functions of each level of Panchayat. Goa has nevertheless undertaken to release its detailed Activity Map imminently. In Andhra Pradesh, Assam, Chattisgarh, Himachal Pradesh, Manipur, Rajasthan and Uttaranchal, the basic ground level work for a detailed activity mapping to give life to their strong Panchayati Raj legislation has been undertaken, but awaits acceptance at the highest level. Bihar and Arunachal Pradesh are also working towards preparing their activity mapping framework. In Madhya Pradesh and Uttar Pradesh, strong action has been taken in the past though excellent report recommending changes are still under the consideration of the Government.

Tripura is going slow in the matter as they have a mix of Sixth Schedule areas and areas covered by Panchayati Raj, which therefore require a judicious approach when devolving activities and responsibilities. In the case of Tamil Nadu, now that the Panchayat elections are over, we anticipate reforms in this direction will commence."It certainly calls for a change in the mindsets.

In order to materialize the concept of 'Empowerment of Panchayats' it should be made mandatory for the States to constitute a Committee each to study Article 243 (G) and the 11th Schedule and make a clear-cut allocation of powers and functions to different tiers of Panchayats in their respective States. Or, an amendment to the Constitution could be brought into to introduce in the Seventh Schedule a list of functions for local Governments, namely, the Panchayats and Municipalities. In other words, it has become necessary to re-examine Schedule and consider introduction of three distinct levels of functions for Union, State and Local Governments.

Panchayati Raj Personnel

Among other factors which have constrained empowerment of panchayats, particularly after the 73rd Amendment Act, relates to the administrative set up necessary to help Panchayats to carry on their functions and responsibilities. In most cases a large-scale deputation has taken place, which has resulted in a lack of effective control by Panchayats over their employees.

In the light of the experience gained, it is necessary that Panchayats may have their own cadre of employees who would work under the full control and supervision of the Panchayats. It implies that Panchayats may have their own service cadre and in the selection to this cadre, weight could be given to the local candidates. In order to materialize this, it will be appropriate that a separate Service

Commission for the Selection of Panchayati Raj Personnel on the lines of the Provincial Services and UPSC be created. Such a Service Commission would have to be governed by the nature, variety and extent of functions and responsibilities assigned to each tier of the Panchayat. The Government may have to consider an amendment to accommodate Panchayat Service in part 14th of the Constitution.

Others

There are a number of other factors, which are also responsible for hindering the process of empowering the panchayats. The experiences from some of the States suggests that the presence of MPs and MLAs in the meetings of various tiers of Panchayats influences the decision-making process, resulting in unhealthy conflicts. The argument given in support is that it does not seem to be logical that MPs and MLAs become a party in the process of decision making in local Self-Government bodies, on whose work and reports they sit in judgment at the State and the National levels. Their presence constrains the process of empowerment. It qualifies for a serious examination as to whether MPs and MLAs should continue to be members of PRIs, and if so, in what capacity!

The District Planning Committees (DPCs) are the only link between the 73rd and the 74th Amendments. The situation with regard to the constitution of DPCs in accordance with the provisions of the Article 243ZD is not very satisfactory. Only few states have dully constituted DPCs and made them significantly operational. (See Annexure-VI for State-wise details on constitution of DPCs). Since DPCs have to play a very important role in preparing a draft plan for the whole district by integrating plans prepared by Panchayats and Municipalities, their composition and functioning becomes very essential. Apart from adequate and effective representation of all the three tiers of panchayats, an attempt should be made to have a common legislation and structure of governance at the district level in order to remove rural-urban dichotomy and to allow effective functioning of the District Planning Committees.

There are a number of institutions, which come in conflict with the district level structure as envisaged under the 73rd Amendment. These include DRDA's, Women's Development Corporations, etc. In essence, these institutions have lost their relevance after the 73rd Amendment came into effect. It is therefore necessary, 'that all such institutions which come in functional conflict with the structures envisaged under 73rd Amendment Act are merged to ensure harmonious integration of different agencies in the service of the common objective of development.'

The 73rd Amendment Act envisages the constitution of State Finance Commissions. The experience suggests that it has proved to be a lengthy process. In some of the cases, the composition of the State Finance Commission is of a kind that in its recommendations it cannot go against the dictates of the respective State Governments. It is, therefore, necessary that the Finance Commissions constituted work within a fixed time-frame. They should examine the gaps between the responsibilities and the requirements of resources for Panchayats at different levels. A formula could be evolved for devolution of finances, which among other considerations, may be based on the population, geographical area of the respective Panchayats, lack of infrastructural facilities and the internal income generation potential of different tiers of Panchayats.

The re-emergence of Panchayati Raj system is an organized response to compulsions and preferences of rural society. With its reactivation, we are witnessing a paradigm shift in development. We shall conclude with a brief discussion on this paradigm shift which is inevitable.

Recent Initiatives

A number of initiatives have been taken recently to place the Panchayats as the central focal point for development of rural areas. These need to be mentioned and commended, irrespective of the fact that they are all government initiatives. These among others include the following:

- The Ministry of Panchayati Raj set up an Expert Group on Grassroots Level Planning under the Chairmanship of Shri V. Ramachandaran. The Group studied the issue of grassroots level planning and set out the steps by which grassroots level planning can be made a reality in time for the Eleventh Five Year Plan. (Annexure VII for constitution and objectives of Expert Group)
- In order to evolve a national consensus through mutual consultation between Centre and States towards preparing a roadmap for Panchayati Raj, Seven Round Tables of State Panchayat Ministers with the Union Minister were convened within 150 days between July-December, 2004. These Round Tables discussed 18 identified dimensions of Panchayati Raj including devolution of functions,funds and functionaries, planning, capacity building and IT-enabled e-governance. (See Annexure VIII for Schedule, location and subjects discussed). Nearly 150 action points comprising the Compendium of Resolutions were unanimously adopted by all the Panchayati Raj Ministers and referred to Chief Ministers for their approval.[3]
- Inspired by the Prime Minister's address to the first Conference of Chief Ministers in June, 2004, the Ministry of Panchayati Raj undertook a major

initiative to promote 'Rural Business Hubs (RBHs)' through the establishment of a governance relationship between business enterprises and Panchayati Raj Institutions. The objective of RBH initiative is to promote at least one Rural Business Hub in each development block of the country by bringing to the attention of business houses, the kind of product or skill available in these blocks which are based on local resources, felt needs and relative absorptive capacity of the local community. The Ministry launched its initiative of Rural Buisness Hubs through Panchayats, at a National Conference in New Delhi on 4th and 5th November, 2004. This National Conference was attended by about 1000 elected representatives of Panchayats at all levels, and 250 business representatives. Several models for establishing linkages between businesses and Panchayats, were presented. It was decided that the Ministry of Panchayati Raj would provide the necessary facilitation to catalyze such collaboration. Key areas appropriate as start-up activity for Rural Business Hubs (RBHs) identified during the conference included decentralized generation and distribution of power, agribusiness and food processing, rural tourism, textiles and handicrafts and Information Technology. The Ministry has so far identified some 850 blocks and their local resources and skill endowments.

- A comprehensive Mid-term Review and Appraisal of the state of the Panchayats in the country in November, 2006. Although these review reports are voluminous, they contain a wealth of information about all the dimensions of Panchayati Raj in the country.

All the above initiatives need to be watched and

observed carefully in the days to come. We are good at taking new initiatives but quite often we lag behind in implementation and follow-up.

Panchayati Raj—Need for a shift in the Development Paradigm [4]

With the reactivation of Panchayati Raj through the 73rd Constitutional Amendment, we have entered a new paradigm of development. Mere existence of Panchayati Raj Institutions or a legal frame-work, however, does not necessarily imply effective participation of their members. Rural people will opt to join in as soon as they realize that the activities that affect the community at large and that, the socio-cultural and economic factors of the community are being given due weight and that they are a part of decision making process. As a UN study points out: "The key to the definition of popular participation as active involvement in decision making is the behaviour of the people and not any particular legal or institutional structure in which the people act."[5]

The rural India is characterized by wide spread poverty and large scale unemployment and under-employment. Though the process of modernization has begun to penetrate India, the rural areas remain mainly 'traditional'. The available resources are even now largely controlled by the elite who constitute a minority of the population. Several primordial structures, such as caste relations, land-based patron-client relations and various cultural practices, permeate the social systems, in rural society, sometimes arresting the process of social change. As a result, we witness, skewed distribution of benefits and uneven development of rural areas. Hence, there is a strong case for people's participation through Panchayati Raj to correct this anomaly. The people's participation in development activities was accepted as a policy imperative and decentralization through reactivation of Panchayati Raj system was to be an important step in this direction. Unfortunately, in practice, it turned to be a strategy of bureaucratic expansion and at some places it resulted into deconcentration of power. Decentralization through Panchayati Raj was essentially conceived as a process of self-governance which allows local decision making as a process that takes place at points close to where the activities are performed, but in effect bureaucratic practices and procedures and the reluctance of the power elite to share power with the people tend to make decentralization in effective.

Bureaucratic indiscretions, including at times those of technocrats, could negate the most well-intended process of democratic decentralization. They have no problems in working under the directions of public representatives at the Central and State levels, but are unable to reconcile with a similar situation at the district and the lower levels. An important dimension of the problem of bureaucracy is that it tends to develop stable action systems which do not lend themselves effectively to coping with the complexity of changing situations in the rural environment. In its efforts to increase efficiency and maintain its supremacy, the bureaucracy becomes concerned largely if not entirely, with technical considerations. Therefore, it is unable to take into account the social considerations of development.[6] If we take a look at the structures meant to effect planning, we notice that in spite of the legal provision in the shape of 'District Planning Committees', they are still centralized in practice, which makes them incomprehensible for a common man. The crucial issue in planning, in so far as it relates to grass-roots level participation at the intermediate and the village panchayat levels, is, not so much of professional competence, as that of the legitimacy, acceptability and relevance of non-professional considerations in the decisions that have to be taken. The bureaucracy at all the three tiers of local governance has to become flexible and beneficiary-oriented rather than remain change-resistant in its operations. Similarly, the political elite have to come out of the fear psychosis of losing their electorate and be ready to share power with local governance representatives. This is perhaps the essence of the new paradigm of development through the Panchayati Raj System.

As the Human Development Report—1993 puts it: "Any proposal to increase people's participation must pass empowerment test—does it increase or decrease people's power to control their lives? This test applies to all institutions that organize or affect human lives."[7] This empowerment test was expected to be materializing through Article 243 G. 'Unfortunately most of the state governments seem to have given limited interpretation to Article 243 G or have chosen to stay within the development domain. Even this development domain leaves a lot to be desired'.[8] There are several conditions which need to be fulfilled if the Panchayats are to pass the empowerment test.

- First, they must have exclusive jurisdiction over their functions and or activities and such functional jurisdiction should be statutorily designed.
- Secondly, the Panchayats should have inherent powers to generate resources in order to enable them to discharge the functions assigned to them.
- Thirdly, one of the cardinal principles of autonomous self-governing institutions is their accountability to the local people. It is necessary to evolve appropriate institutional forums to ensure accountability of Panchayats to the people. Gram Sabha is one such institution. But this is not enough. New kinds of institutional forums would be

necessary to ensure accountability of Panchayats, particularly at the Panchayat Samiti and Zila Parishad levels.

- Fourthly, many Central and State Acts have provisions which conflict with the spirit of the 73rd Amendment. A hard look at their provisions is necessary to correct the anomaly.
- Finally, in order to be autonomous self-governing institutions, Panchayats should have control over their instrumentalities and, as such, restructuring of district bureaucracy has become an urgent task. The goal of setting up institutional self-government for rural areas will remain a pipe dream, unless serious thought is given to the issue of restructuring the field-level bureaucracy of the state governments.

All the above indicate a shift in the development paradigm through Panchayati Raj which is inevitable.

References

[1] Veledictory Address delivered by Shri Mani Shankar Aiyer, Minister for Panchayati Raj, Govt. of India on 26 February, 2006 during GNLG meeting at Institute of Social Sciences, New Delhi.

[2] Panchayati Raj in the States- Chapter-IV The State of Panchayats—A Mid-Term Review and Appraisal, Ministry of Panchayati Raj, Govt. of India November, 2006 pp71-72.

[3] For details about 150 resolutions, refer '*A Compendium of Resolutions of the Seven Round Tables of Ministers In-Charge of Panchayati Raj*' July-December, 2004, Ministry of Panchayati Raj, Govt of India.

[4] This section is a modified version of the write up prepared by the author for 'Revitalization of Panchayati Raj in India- Problems and Prospects' RGF, op. cit p. 7-9.

[5] "Popular participation in Decision Making for Development", UN New York, 1973, p. 7.

[6] See CIRDAP, 1984, "People's participation in Rural Development", in An overview of South and South-East Asian Countries compiled by the author.

[7] "Popular participation in Decision Making for Development", UN New York, 1973, p. 7.

[8] Panchayati Raj Development Report—1995, Institute of Social Sciences, New Delhi.

Annexure-I

Panchayati Raj: A historic step

Jawaharlal Nehru

We are going to lay foundations of democracy or Panchayati Raj in our country.

Rajasthan is the heart of India, historically as well as geographically. The people of Rajasthan, who live in village and towns, have pledged themselves to take upon themselves the heavy responsibilities of democracy and the Government of this State has, by an Act of Legislature, handed over the responsibilities to the people. It is a historic event. It is fitting that the programme of Panchayati Raj should be inaugurated on Mahatma Gandhi's birthday.

After we became independent we established the rule of the people. Every citizen of India was given the right of vote. The people enjoyed the right to elect their representatives to the State Legislatures and to Lok Sabha. It was a step in the right direction, but real democracy did not come into being with it. India will make progress only when the people living in the villages become politically conscious. The progress of our country is bound up with the progress in our villages. If our villages make progress, India will become a strong nation and nobody will be able to stop its onward march.

It was seven years ago that we started this great movement with the Community Projects and the National Extension Service. These have by now covered more than three lakh villages. On the whole good work has been done. But we have not been able to do as much as we expected. The reason for our slow progress is our dependence on official machinery. An officer, who is an expert, may help but development work can be executed only if the people take the responsibility in their own hands. Some people thought that if the responsibility was handed over to the people, they would probably not be able to shoulder it. But it is only by providing opportunity to the people that they can be trained to shoulder responsibilities. It become imperative that a bold step be taken whereby more and more responsibility could be transferred to the people. The people were not merely to be consulted but effective power was to be entrusted to them.

Therefore, we decided that in every village there should be a village panchayat with more powers, as also a co-operative society which will help its economic effort.

The panchayat is to help in the day-to-day administration of the village and the co-operative is to manage its economic affairs. The responsibilities of administration should not be only in the hands of big officials but should be divided among our 400 million people. We should bring the people together to act in co-operation and in consultation with each other.

The third important institution which we need in our village is the school. Every village should have a school so that the villagers should be able to receive education. And women should get equal opportunities for education.

We are now in our Second Five Year Plan. It will come to an end after a year or so. The Third Five Year Plan is in the making. The time has come when the responsibility for planning and executing development schemes should be entrusted to the people. I shall, therefore ask you to shoulder such responsibility with faith and courage. The people of India are looking towards you. I am fully confident that not only in Rajasthan but in every part of India where responsibility is entrusted to the people, it will yield happy results.

You have taken a historic step on an auspicious day and I congratulate you and offer my good wishes. You should try to make your panchayats a success.

Formerly in India the maharajas and their people were divided into water-tight compartments but now the distinction between the rulers and the ruled has been removed. Nevertheless sometimes our officers consider themselves to be masters. I hope that your presidents, sarpanches and other officers will not function in that way. An officer who becomes overbearing and employs bureaucratic methods will not be able to win the co-operation of the people. A good officer works in a spirit of equality. It is only then that he can train others. You should work in mutual co-operation. In political life everyone has a vote; in economic matters everyone has equal opportunities; in our panchayats also everyone should be considered equal; there should be no distinction between man and woman, high and low. We have to march ahead in a spirit of unity and brotherhood and with faith in our work and ourselves.

The world is watching you. If you flinch from your determination and get involved in mutual quarrels and petty factions, you will not be able to succeed in your mission. You have to awaken the masses of Rajasthan, and it will be a great step. The future generations will be able to say with pride that you laid the solid foundations of democracy.

Source: From the speech delivered by Pt. Jawahar Lal Nehru in Hindi at Nagaur in Rajasthan on the occasion of the inauguration of Panchayati Raj in the State, October 2, 1959, which appeared in *Kurukshetra,* Vol.XXXVII No.5, February, 1989.

Annexure-II

Milestones in the Evolution of Local Government since Independence

Towards First Generation Panchayats

1948-49	Constituent Assembly debates on the role of Panchayati Raj in Indian polity
1950	The Constitution of India comes into force on 26 January; Directive Principles of State Policy mention village panchayats as 'units of self-government' (Art. 40)
1952	Community Development Programme starts on 2 October
1957	Balvantrai Mehta Committee, appointed in January, submits its report on 24 November
1958-60	Several state governments enact new Panchayat Acts bringing in three-tier panchayat system
1959	Jawaharlal Nehru inaugurates the first generation panchayat at Nagaur in Rajasthan on 2 October Kerala District Council Bill is introduced in Kerala Assembly; lapses after Assembly is dissolved
1964-77	Decline of first generation Panchayati Raj Institutions

Growth and Decline of Second Generation Panchayats

1978	Panchayat elections are held in West Bengal on party basis on 4 June—marking the beginning of second generation of Panchayati Raj Asoka Mehta Committee on working of panchayats, appointed on 12 December 1977, submits its report on 21 August
1983	Karnataka government enacts new PR Act
1984	Hanumantha Rao Committee on district level planning, appointed by Planning Commission in September 1982, submits its report in May
1985	Karnataka PR Act receives President's assent in July; comes into force on 14 August

1985	G.V.K. Rao Committee on administrative aspects of rural development, appointed by Planning Commission on 25 March, submits its report in December
1986	Andhra Pradesh follows West Bengal and Karnataka Panchayati Raj model
1987	Karnataka holds panchayat elections in January
1990-92	Panchayats are dissolved and brought under administrators in Karnataka

Constitutionalisation of Panchayati Raj

1986	L.M. Singhvi Committee submits its report on 27 November; recommends constitutional status for panchayats
1988	Parliament Consultative Committee appoints a sub-committee under chairpersonship of P. K. Thungan to consider Constitutional Amendment
1989	64th Constitutional Amendment Bill is introduced in Parliament on 15 May; is defeated in Rajya Sabha on 15 October
1990	74th Constitution Amendment Bill is introduced in Parliament on 7 September; lapses on dissolution of Lok Sabha
1991	72nd (Panchayats) and 73rd (Municipalities) Amendment Bills are introduced in Parliament; referred to the Parliament's Joint Select Committee in September
1992	Lok Sabha passes both the Bills on 22 December; Rajya Sabha passes them on 23 December
1993	73rd Amendment Act, 1992 comes into force on 24 April 74th Amendment Act, 1992 comes into force on 1 June
1993-94	All state governments pass Conformity Acts between 30 May 1993 and 23 April, 1994
1994	Madhya Pradesh holds panchayat elections under the 73rd Amendment dispensation on 30 May
1996	Provisions of the Panchayats (Extension to the Scheduled Areas) Act, 1996, extending 73rd Amendment Act to Scheduled Areas, comes into force on 24 December. Kerala launches People's Plan Campaign on 16 August
2001	Bihar holds panchayat elections after 23 years (11-30 April)

2001 83rd Constitution Amendment Act, 2000 amends Art. 243 M to dispense with reservations for Scheduled Castes in Arunachal Pradesh—paving way for panchayat elections in the only state yet to hold them under the new dispensation

Source: Panchayati Raj Update, October, 2002, Institute of Social Sciences, New Delhi.

Annexure-III

The Constitution (Seventy-Third Amendment) Act, 1992

Statement of Objects and Reasons appended to the Constitution (Seventy-second Amendment) Bill, 1991 which was enacted as the Constitution (Seventy-third Amendment) Act, 1992

Statement of Objects and Reasons

1. Though the Panchayati Raj Institutions have been in existence for a long time, it has been observed that these institutions have not been able to acquire the status and dignity of viable and responsive people's bodies due to a number of reasons including absence of regular elections, prolonged super sessions, insufficient representation of weaker sections like Scheduled Castes, Scheduled Tribes and women, inadequate devolution of powers and lack of financial resources.
2. Article 40 of the Constitution which enshrines one of the Directive Principles of State Policy lays down that the State shall take steps to organize Village Panchayats and endow them with such powers and authority as may be necessary to enable them to function as units of self-government. In the light of the experience in the last forty years and in view of the short-comings which have been observed, it is considered that there is an imperative need to enshrine in the Constitution certain basic and essential features of Panchayati Raj Institutions to impact certainty, continuity and strength to them.
3. Accordingly, it is proposed to add a new part relating to Panchayats in the Constitution to provide for among other things, Gram Sabha in a village or group of villages; constitution of Panchayats at village and other level or levels; direct elections to all seats in Panchayats at the village and intermediate level, if any, and to the offices of Chairpersons of Panchayats at such levels; reservation of seats for the Scheduled Castes and Scheduled Tribes in proportion to their population for

membership of Panchayats and office of Chairpersons in Panchayats at each level; reservation of not less than one-third of the seats for women; fixing tenure of 5 years for Panchayats and holding elections within a period of 6 months in the event of suppression of any Panchayat; disqualifications for membership of Panchayats; devolution by the State Legislature of powers and responsibilities upon the Panchayats with respect to the preparation of plans for economic developments and social justice and for the implementation of development schemes; sound finance of the Panchayats by securing authorization from State Legislatures for grants-in-aid to the Panchayats from the Consolidated Fund of the State, as also assignment to, or appropriation by, the Panchayats of the revenues of designated taxes, duties, tolls and fees; setting up of a Finance Commission within one year of the proposed amendment and thereafter every 5 years to review the financial position of Panchayats; auditing of accounts of the Panchayats; powers of State Legislatures to make provisions with respect to elections to Panchayats under the superintendence, direction and control of the chief electoral officer of the State; application of the provisions of the said part to union territories; excluding certain States and areas from the application of the provisions of the said part; continuance of existing laws and Panchayats until one year from the commencement of the proposed amendment and barring interference by courts in electoral matters relating to Panchayats.

4. The Bill seeks to achieve the aforesaid objectives.

New Delhi — G. VENKAT SWAMY
The 10th September, 1991

THE CONSTITUTION (SEVENTY-THIRD AMENDMENT) ACT, 1992

[20th April, 1993]

An Act further to amend the Constitution of India.

Be it enacted by Parliament in the Forty-third Year of the Republic of India as follows:

1) Short title and commencement this Act may be called the Constitution (Seventy-third Amendment) Act, 1992(2). It shall come into force on such date as the Central Government may, by notification in the Official Gazette, appoint.
2) Insertion of new Part IX—After Part VIII of the Constitution, the following Part shall be inserted, namely.

PART IX

THE PANCHAYATS

Definitions—In this Part, unless the context otherwise requires:

a) "District" means a district in a State;
b) "Gram Sabha" means a body consisting of persons registered in the electoral rolls relating to a village comprised within the area of Panchayat at the village level;
c) "Intermediate level" means a level between the village and district levels specified by the Governor of a State by public notification to be the intermediate level for the purposes of this Part;
d) "Panchayat" means an institution (by whatever name called) of self-government constituted under article 243 B, for the rural areas;
e) "Panchayat area"means the territorial area of a Panchayat;
f) "Population" means the population as ascertained at the last preceding census of which the relevant figures have been published;
g) "Village" means a village specified by the Governor by public notification to be a village for the purposes of this Part and includes a group of villages so specified.

Gram Sabha—A Gram Sabha may exercise such powers and perform such functions at the village level as the Legislature of a State may, by law, provide.

Constitution of Panchayats—

1) There shall be constituted in every State, Panchayats at the village, intermediate and district levels in accordance with the provisions of this Part.
2) Notwithstanding anything in clause (1) Panchayats at the

intermediate level may not be constituted in a State having a population not exceeding twenty lakhs.

Composition of Panchayats—

1) Subject to the provisions of this Part, the Legislature of a State may, by law, make provisions with respect to the composition of Panchayats—provided that the ratio between the population of the territorial area of a Panchayat at any level and the number of seats in such Panchayat to be filled by election shall, so far as practicable, be the same throughout the State.
2) All the seats in a Panchayat shall be filled by persons chosen by direct election from territorial constituencies in the Panchayat area and; for this purpose, each Panchayat area shall be divided into territorial constituencies in such manner that the ratio between the population of each constituency and the number of seats allotted to it shall, so far as practicable, be the same throughout the Panchayat area.
3) The Legislature of a State may, by law, provide for the representation:
   a) of the Chairpersons of the Panchayats at the village level, in the Panchayats at the intermediate level or, in the case of a State not having Panchayats at the intermediate level, in the Pancayats at the district level;
   b) of the Chairpersons of the Panchayats at the intermediate level, in the Panchayats at the district level;
   c) of the members of the House of the People and the members of the Legislative Assembly of the State representing constituencies which comprise wholly or partly a Panchayat area at a level other than the village level, in such Panchayat;
   d) of the members of the Council of States and the members of the Legislative Council of the State, where they are registered as electors within—
      (i) a Panchayat area at the intermediate level, in Panchayat at the intermediate level;
      (ii) a Panchayat area at the district level, in Panchayat at the district level.
4) The Chairperson of a Panchayat and other members of a Panchayat where constituencies in the Panchayat area shall have the right to vote in the meetings of the Panchayats.

5) The Chairperson of—
   a) a Panchayat at the village level shall be elected in such manner as the Legislature of a State may, by law, provide; and
   b) a Panchayat at the intermediate level or district level shall be elected by, and from amongst, the elected members thereof.

Reservation of seats—

1) Seats shall be reserved for
   a) the Scheduled Castes; and
   b) the Scheduled Tribes

   In every Panchayat the number of seats of reserved shall bear, as nearly as may be, the same proportion to the total number of seats to be filled by direct election in that Panchayat as the population of the Scheduled Castes in that Panchayat area or of the Scheduled Tribes in that Panchayat area bears to the total population of that area and such seats may be allotted by rotation to different constituencies in a Panchayat.
2) Not less than one-third of the total number of seats reserved under clause (1) shall be reserved for women belonging to the Scheduled Castes or, as the case may be, the Scheduled Tribes.
3) Not less than one-third (including the number of seats reserved for women belonging to the Scheduled Castes and the Scheduled Tribes) of the total number of seats to be filled by direct election in every Panchayat shall be reserved for women and such seats may be allotted by rotation to different constituencies in a Panchayat.
4) The offices of the Chairpersons in the Panchayats at the village or any other level shall be reserved for the Scheduled Castes, the Scheduled Tribes and women in such manner as the Legislature of a State may, by law, provide—

   Provided that the number of offices of Chairpersons reserved for the Scheduled Castes and the Scheduled Tribes in the Panchayats at each level in any State shall bear, as nearly as may be, the same proportion to the total number of such offices in the Panchayats at each level as the population of the Scheduled Castes in the State or of the Scheduled Tribes in the State bears to the total population of the State;

Provided further that not less than one-third of the total number of offices of Chairpersons in the Panchayats at each level shall be reserved for women;

Provided also that the number of offices reserved under this clause shall be allotted by rotation to different Panchayats at each level.

5) The reservation of seats under clauses (1) and (2) and the reservation of offices of Chairpersons (other than the reservation for women) under clause (4) shall cease to have effect on the expiration of the period specified in article 334.
6) Nothing in this Part shall prevent the Legislature of a State from making any provision for reservation of seats in any Panchayat or offices of Chairpersons in the Panchayats at any level in favour of backward class of citizens.

Duration of Panchayats etc.—

1) Every Panchayat, unless sooner dissolved under any law for the time being in force, shall continue for five years from the date appointed for its first meeting and no longer.
2) No amendment of any law for the time being in force shall have the effect of causing dissolution of a Panchayat at any level, which is functioning immediately before such amendment, till the expiration of its duration specified in clause (1).
3) An election to constitute a Panchayat shall be completed—
   a) before the expiry of its duration specified in clause (1);
   b) before the expiration of a period of six months from the date of its dissolution.

      Provided that where the remainder of the period for which the dissolved Panchayat would have continued is less than six months, it shall not be necessary to hold any election under this clause for constituting the Panchayat for such period.
4) A Panchayat constituted upon the dissolution of a Panchayat before the expiration of its duration shall continue only for the remainder of the period for which the dissolved Panchayat would have continued under clause (1) had it not been so dissolved.

Disqualifications for membership—

1) A person shall be disqualified for being chosen as, and for

being, a member of a Panchayat—

a) if he is so disqualified by or under any law for the time being in force for the purposes of elections to the Legislature of the State concerned.

   Provided that no person shall be disqualified on the ground that he is less than twenty-five years of age, if he has attained the age of twenty-one years;

b) if he is so disqualified by or under any law made by the Legislature of the State.

2) If any question arises as to whether a member of a Panchayat has become subject to any of the disqualifications mentioned in clause (1), the question shall be referred for the decision of such authority and in such manner as the Legislature of a State may, by law, provide.

Powers, authority and responsibilities of Panchayats—

Subject to the provisions of this Constitution, the Legislature of a State may, by law, endow the Panchayats with such powers and authority as may be necessary to enable them to function as institutions of self-government and such law may contain provisions for the devolution of powers and responsibilities upon Panchayats at the appropriate level, subject to such conditions as may be specified therein, with respect to—

a) the preparation of plans for economic development and social justice;

b) the implementation of schemes for economic development and social justice as may be entrusted to them including those in relation to the matters listed in the Eleventh Schedule.

Powers to impose taxes by, and Funds of, the Panchayats—

The Legislature of a State may, by law—

a) authorize a Panchayat to levy, collect and appropriate such taxes, duties, tolls and fees in accordance with such procedure and subject to such limits;

b) assign to a Panchayat such taxes, duties, tolls and fees levied and collected by the State Government for such purposes and subject to such conditions and limits;

c) provide for making such grants-in-aid to the Panchayats from the Consolidated Fund of the State; and

d) provide for constitution of such Funds for crediting all moneys received, respectively, by or on behalf of the Panchayats and also for the withdrawal of such moneys there from, as may be specified in the law.

Constitution of Finance Commission to review financial position—

1) The Governor of a State shall, as soon as may be within one year from the commencement of the Constitution (Seventy-third Amendment) Act, 1992, and thereafter at the expiration of every fifth year, constitute a Finance Commission to review the financial position of the Panchayats and to make recommendations to the Governor as to—
   a) the principles which should govern—
      (i) the distribution between the State and the Panchayats of the net proceeds of the taxes, duties, tolls and fees leviable by the State, which may be divided between them under this Part and the allocation between the Panchayats at all levels of their respective shares of such proceeds;
      (ii) the determination of the taxes, duties, tolls and fees which may be assigned to, or appropriated by, the Panchayat;
      (iii) the grants-in-aid to the Panchayats from the Consolidated Fund of the State;
   b) the measures needed to improve the financial position of the Panchayats;
   c) any other matter referred to the Finance Commission by the Governor in the interests of sound finance of the Panchayats.
2) The Legislature of a State may, by law, provide for the composition of the Commission, the qualifications which shall be requisite for appointment as members thereof and the manner in which they shall be selected.
3) The Commission shall determine their procedure and shall have such powers in the performance of their functions as the Legislature of the State may, by law, confer on them.
4) The Governor shall cause every recommendation made by the Commission under this article together with an explanatory memorandum as to the action taken thereon to be laid before the Legislature of the State.

Audit of accounts of Panchayats—

The Legislature of a State may, by law, make provisions with respect to the maintenance of accounts by the Panchayats and the auditing of such accounts.

Elections to the Panchayats—

1) The superintendence, direction and control of the preparation of electoral rolls for, and the conduct of, all elections to the Panchayats shall be vested in a State Election Commission consisting of a State Election Commissioner to be appointed by the Governor.
2) Subject to the provisions of any law made by the Legislature of a State, the conditions of service and tenure of office of the State Election Commissioner shall be such as the Governor may by rule determine:
   Provided that the State Election Commissioner shall not be removed from his office except in like manner and on the like grounds as a Judge of a High Court and the conditions of service of the State Election Commissioner shall not be varied to his disadvantage after his appointment.
3) The Governor of a State shall, when so requested by the State Election Commission, make available to the State Election Commission such staff as may be necessary for the discharge of the functions conferred on the State Election Commission by clause (1).
4) Subject to the provisions of this Constitution, the Legislature of a State may, by law, make provision with respect to all matters relating to, or in connection with, elections to the Panchayats.

Application to Union territories—

The provisions of this Part shall apply to the Union territories and shall, in their application to a Union territory, have effect as if the references to the Governor of a State were references to the Administrator of the Union Territory appointed under article 239 and references to the Legislature or the Legislative Assembly of a State were references, in relation to a Union territory having a Legislative Assembly, to that Legislative Assembly—

Provided that the President may, by public notification, direct that the provisions of this Part shall apply to any Union territory or part thereof subject to such exceptions and modifications as he may specify in the notification.

Part not to apply to certain areas—

1) Nothing in this Part shall apply to the Scheduled Areas referred to in clause (1), and the tribal areas referred to in clause (2), of article 244.
2) Nothing in this Part shall apply to—
   a) the States of Nagaland, Meghalaya and Mizoram;
   b) the Hill Areas in the State of Manipur for which District Councils exist under any law for the time being in force.
3) Nothing in this Part—
   a) relating to Panchayats at the district level shall apply to the hill areas of the district of Darjeeling in the State of West Bengal for which Darjeeling Gorkha Hill Council exists under any law for the time being in force;
   b) shall be construed to affect the functions and powers of the Darjeeling Gorkha Hill Council constituted under such law.
4) Notwithstanding anything in this Constitution—
   a) the Legislature of a State referred to in sub-clause (a) of clause (2) may, by law, extend this Part to that State, except the areas, if any, referred to in clause (1), if the Legislative Assembly of that State passes a resolution to that effect by a majority of the total membership of that House and by a majority of not less than two-thirds of the members of that House present and voting;
   b) Parliament may, by law, extend the provisions of this Part to the Scheduled Areas and the tribal areas referred to in clause (1) subject to such exceptions and modifications as may be specified in such law, and no such law shall be deemed to be an amendment of this Constitution for the purposes of article 368.

Continuance of existing laws and Panchayats—

Notwithstanding anything in this Part, any provision of any law relating to Panchayats in force in a State immediately before the commencement of the Constitution (Seventy-third Amendment) Act, 1992, which is inconsistent with the provisions of this Part, shall continue to be in force until amended or repealed by a competent Legislature or other competent authority or until the expiration of one year from such commencement, whichever is earlier—

Provided that all the Panchayats existing immediately before such commencement shall continue till the expiration of their duration, unless sooner dissolved by a resolution passed to that effect by the Legislative Assembly of that State or, in the case of a State having a Legislative Council, by each House of the Legislature of that State.

Bar to interference by courts in electoral matters— Notwithstanding anything in this Constitution, (a) the validity of any law relating to the delimitation of constituencies or the allotment of seats to such constituencies, made or purporting to be made under article 243K, shall not be called in question in any court; (b) no election to any Panchayat shall be called in question except by an election petition presented to such authority and in such manner as is provided for by or under any law made by the Legislature of a State.

Amendment of article 280—In clause (3) of article 280 of the Constitution, after sub-clause (b), the following sub-clause shall be inserted, namely:

"(bb) the measures needed to augment the Consolidated Fund of a State to supplement the resources of the Panchayats in the State on the basis of the recommendations made by the Finance Commission of the State".

Amendment of Eleventh Schedule—After the Tenth Schedule to the.Constitution the following Schedule shall be added, namely:

ELEVENTH SCHEDULE

(Article 243G)

1. Agriculture, including agricultural extension.
2. Land improvement, implementation of land reforms, land consolidation and soil conservation.
3. Minor irrigation, water management and water-shed development.
4. Animal husbandry, dairying and poultry.
5. Fisheries.

6. Social forestry and farm forestry.
7. Minor forest produce.
8. Small scale industries, including food processing industries.
9. Khadi, village and cottage industries.
10. Rural housing.
11. Drinking water.
12. Fuel and fodder.
13. Roads, culverts, bridges, ferries, waterways and other means of communication.
14. Rural electrification, including distribution of electricity.
15. Non-conventional energy sources.
16. Poverty alleviation programme.
17. Education, including primary and secondary schools.
18. Technical training and vocational education.
19. Adult and non-formal education.
20. Libraries.
21. Cultural activities.
22. Markets and fairs.
23. Health and sanitation, including hospitals, primary health centres and dispensaries.
24. Family welfare.
25. Women and child development.
26. Social welfare, including welfare of the handicapped and mentally retarded.
27. Welfare of the weaker sections, and in particular, of the Scheduled Castes and the Scheduled Tribes.
28. Public distribution system.
29. Maintenance of community assets.

(*Source:* National Panchayat Portal, Ministry of Panchayati Raj, Govt. of India)

Annexure- IV

THE PROVISIONS OF THE PANCHAYATS (EXTENSION TO THE SCHEDULED AREAS) ACT, 1996 No. 40 OF 1996

(24th December, 1996)

An Act to provide for the extension of the provisions of Part IX of the Constitution relating to the Panchayats to the Scheduled Areas.

Be it enacted by Parliament in the Forty-seventh Year of the Republic of India as follows:

Short title

1. This Act may be called the Provisions of the Panchayats (Extension to the Scheduled Areas) Act, 1996

Definition

2. In this Act, unless the context otherwise requires, "Scheduled Areas" means the Scheduled Areas as referred to in Clause (1) of Article 244 of the Constitution.

Extension of Part IX of the Constitution

3. The provision of Part IX of the Constitution relating to Panchayats are hereby extended to the Scheduled Areas subject to such exceptions and modifications as are provided in section 4.

Exceptions and modifications to Part IX of the Constitution

4. Notwithstanding anything contained under Part IX of the Constitution, the Legislature of a State shall not make any law under that Part which is inconsistent with any of the following features, namely:
   a) a State legislation on the Panchayats that may be made shall be in consonance with the customary law, social and religious practices and traditional management practices of community resources;

b) a village shall ordinarily consist of a habitation or a group of habitations or a hamlet or a group of hamlets comprising a community and managing its affairs in accordance with traditions and customs;
c) every village shall have a Gram Sabha consisting of persons whose names are included in the electoral rolls for the Panchayat at the village level;
d) every Gram Sabha shall be competent to safeguard and preserve the traditions and customs of the people, their cultural identity, community resources and the customary mode of dispute resolution;
e) every Gram Sabha shall—
    (i) approve of the plans, programmes and projects for social and economic development before such plans, programmes and projects are taken up for implementation by the Panchayat at the village level;
    (ii) be responsible for the identification or selection of persons as beneficiaries under the poverty alleviation and other programmes;
f) every Panchayat at the village level shall be required to obtain from the Gram Sabha a certification of utilisation of funds by that Panchayat for the plans, programmes and projects referred to in clause (e);
g) the reservation of seats in the Scheduled Areas at every Panchayat shall be in proportion to the population of the communities in that Panchayat for whom reservation is sought to be given under Part IX of the Constitution—
Provided that the reservation for the Scheduled Tribes shall not be less than one-half of the total number of seats;
Provided further that all seats of Chairpersons of Panchayats at all levels shall be reserved for the Scheduled Tribes;
h) the State Government may nominate persons belonging to such Scheduled Tribes as have no representation in the Panchayat at the intermediate level or the Panchayat at the district level—
Provided that such nomination shall not exceed one-tenth of the total members to be elected in that Panchayat;
i) the Gram Sabha or the Panchayats at the appropriate level shall be consulted before making the acquisition of land in the Scheduled Areas for development projects and

before re-setling or rehabilitating persons affected by such projects in the Scheduled Areas; the actual planning and implementation of the projects in the Scheduled Areas shall be coordinated at the State level;

j) planning and management of minor water bodies in the Scheduled Areas shall be entrusted to Panchayats at the appropriate level;

k) the recommendations of the Gram Sabha or the Panchayats at the appropriate level shall be made mandatory prior to grant of prospecting licence or mining lease for minor minerals in the Scheduled Areas;

l) the prior recommendation of the Gram Sabha or the Panchayats at the appropriate level shall be made mandatory for grant of concession for the exploitation of minor minerals by auction;

m) while endowing Panchayats in the Scheduled Areas with such powers and authority as may be necessary to enable them to function as institutions of self-government, a State Legislature shall ensure that the Panchayats at the appropriate level and the Gram Sabha are endowed specifically with—

   (i) the power to enforce prohibition or to regulate or restrict the sale and consumption of any intoxicant;
   (ii) the ownership of minor forest produce;
   (iii) the power to prevent alienation of land in the Scheduled Areas and to take appropriate action to restore any unlawfully alienated land of a Scheduled Tribe;
   (iv) the power to manage village markets by whatever name called;
   (v) the power to exercise control over money lending to the Scheduled Tribes;
   (vi) the power to exercise control over institutions and functionaries in all social sectors;
   (vii) the power to control over local plans and resources for such plans including tribal sub-plans;

n) the State Legislations that may endow Panchayats with powers and authority as may be necessary to enable them to function as institutions of self-government shall contain safeguards to ensure that Panchayats at the higher level do not assume the powers and authority of any Panchayat at the lower level or of the Gram Sabha;

o) the State Legislature shall endeavour to follow the pattern of the Sixth Schedule to the Constitution while designing the administrative arrangements in the Panchayats at district levels in the Scheduled Areas.

Continuance of existing laws on panchayats—

5. Notwithstanding anything in Part IX of the Constitution with exceptions and modifications made by this Act, any provision of any law relating to Panchayats in force in the Scheduled Areas, immediately before the date on which this act receives the assent of the President, which is inconsistent with the provisions of Part IX with such exceptions and modifications shall continue to be in force until amended or repealed by a competent Legislature or other competent authority or until the expiration of one year from the date on which this Act receives the assent of the President;

   Provided that all the Panchayats existing immediately before such date shall continue till the expiration of their duration unless sooner dissolved by a resolution passed to that effect by the Legislative Assembly of that State or, in the case of a State having Legislative Council, by each House of the Legislature of that State.

Sd/-
K.L. MOHANPURIA
Secy. to the Govt. of India

(*Source:* National Panchayat Portal, Ministry of Panchayati Raj, Govt. of India)

Annexure-V

Extracts from reports of various committees on PRIs

I. Balvantrai Mehta Committee: 1957

PANCHAYATI RAJ: CONCEPT AND APPROACH

To us in this country, the term 'community development' is of recent origin. We have so far used such terms as rural development, constructive work, adult education and rural uplift to denote certain of its aspects. The word "Community" has for the past many decades, denoted religious or caste groups or, in some instances, economic groups not necessarily living in one locality; but with the inauguration of the community development programme in this country, it is intended to apply it to the concept of the village community as a whole, cutting across caste, religious and economic differences. It is a programme which emphasizes that the interest in the development of the locality is necessarily and unavoidably common to all the people living there. The Planning Commission, in their First Five-Year Plan, described community development as the "method through which the Five Year Plan seeks to initiate a process of transformation of the social and economic life of the villages". This method is to process the development of the area through people's own democratic and cooperative organizations, with the Government helping only with technical advice, supplies and credit. It is "designed to promote better living for whole community with the active participation and, if possible, on the initiative of the community; but if this initiative is not forthcoming, by the same use of techniques for arousing and stimulating it in order to secure its active and enthusiastic response".

While operating through the people's local organizations, the programme simultaneously strengthens the foundations of democracy on which our Constitution stands, by making the villager understand the significance of development and his own position in the process of development, and it makes him realize his position in this vast democracy. Thus, community development and democracy progress through and strengthen each other. The community projects are of vital importance "not so much for the material achievement that they would bring about but much more so, because they seem to build up the community and the individual and to make the latter the builder of his own village centres and of India in the larger sense".

In this community development "the role of the Government is to plan and organize the programmes on a national basis according to a well-conceived policy and secondly, to provide the technical service and basic material which go beyond the resources of the communities and of the voluntary organization. In relation to the people, community development is essentially both an educational and organizational process. It is educational because it is concerned with changing such attitudes and practices as are obstacles to social and economic improvements, engendering particular attitudes which are conducive to these improvements and more generally, promoting a greater receptivity to change. It is organizational not only because people acting together are better able to pursue the interests which they have in common but also because it requires the reorientation of existing institutions or the creation of new types of institutions to make self-help fully effective and to provide the necessary channels for governmental services. To be fully effective, this demands the emergence and training of a new type of local leaders. The value of organizing the people consists not only in the help which it may give towards achieving particular concrete results, but also in the general contribution which it may make towards increasing social coherence.

"Implementation of community development programme on a national scale requires—adoption of consistent policies, specific administrative arrangements, recruitment and training of personnel, mobilization of local and national resources and organizational or research, experimentation and evaluation.... A programme of community development is most successful when it becomes an integral part of, or is closely related to, the existing administrative organization at the local, intermediate and national levels".

The Planning Commission in the First Five Year Plan referred to rural extension as the agency for the transformation of the social and economic life of the villages. It must, therefore, be borne in mind that the national extension service, as it is called, is nothing more than a staffing pattern. It is an agency for extending to the villagers the scientific and technical knowledge in certain fields like agriculture, animal husbandry and the rural industry. The extension agency also includes an element of service agency, e.g., for taking preventive and prophylactic measures like inoculation and vaccination, but it must never forget its essential role of extension. Its main function is to make the people understand what change or innovation will benefit them, why it will benefit them and how it can be introduced. It is for the community to participate in all the activities which will lead to such change or innovation. Here, the term participation assumes some significance. People's participation is not merely their providing a certain proportion of the cost of a particular work in cash, kind or manual labour. It is their full realisation that all aspects of community development are their concern and the Government's participation is only to assist them where such assistance is necessary. It is the gradual development of their faith in the efficacy of their own cooperative action in solving their local problems. This attitude can be developed by close mutual cooperation between the different sections of the community. Such participation is possible only through the organisation of cooperative institutions and of elective democratic institutions.

During the past few years plans for community development have often been attempted to be processed not through such democratic institution but through ad hoc bodies like Vikas Mandals etc. Often, we have been told that the village panchayat is for various reasons not suitable for such work. This is a confession not merely of our lack of faith in democracy but of our failure to make the programme a genuine community development programme. It can become genuine only by operating through the cooperatives on the one hand and the statutory elective representative bodies on the other.

The backward community has to develop on so many different lines and its felt needs are so numerous and so fast growing that with the limitations of the available resources, it has to prescribe for itself certain priorities. In a large country which is planning its overall development, the development of the community has to be integrated with the development of the country as a whole. Such integration will need that the overall priorities should be prescribed by the Government and the details worked out by the village community. The three main directions in which community development programme should work are—"First, increased employment and increased production by the application of scientific methods of agriculture, including horticulture, animal husbandry, fisheries, etc. and the establishment of subsidiary and cottage industries; secondly, self-help and self-reliance and the largest possible extension of the principle of cooperation; and thirdly, the need for devoting a portion of the vast unutilized time and energy in the countryside for the benefit of the community". For obvious reasons, economic development has to take precedence over welfare activities. But in an active democratic State the latter cannot be completely neglected because of the demands of the former.

We have examined this matter in some detail. Some of our detailed conclusions appear in the later sections. Here we would point out that the tendency in the past years has been to stress the welfare activities more than the economic development activities. This is because the former are popular, easy of achievement and impress the casual observer; the villager himself, often unable to understand even the meaning of terms Community Development and National Extension Service, as translated into his own language, gives a full measure of his admiration and gratitude for the people who have brought him these amenities. We would urge that the emphasis should shift without delay to the more demanding aspects of economic development. The priorities as between the different activities should be—supply of drinking water, improvement of agriculture and animal husbandry, cooperative activities, rural industry and health followed by all others. The allocation of priorities is, however, not intended to operate by way of absolute precedence, but to indicate a greater concentration on certain items of work and less on others without totally excluding the latter. An intensive programme of economic development will generate a demand for a programme of amenities. We are of the view that greater stress on the former, especially in the initial stages, will gradually lead to the latter.

DEMOCRATIC DECENTRALISATION

Admittedly, one of the least successful aspects of the C.D. & N.E.S. work is its attempt to evoke popular initiative. We have found that few of the local bodies at a level higher than the village panchayat have shown any enthusiasm or interest in this work; and even the panchayats have not come into the field to any appreciable extent. An attempt has been made to harness local initiative through the formation of ad hoc bodies mostly with nominated personnel and invariably advisory in character. These bodies have so far given neither indication of durable strength nor the leadership necessary to provide the motive force for continuing the improvement of economic and social condition in rural areas. So long as we do not discover or create a representative and democratic institution which will supply the "local interest, supervision and care necessary to ensure that expenditure of money upon local objects conforms with the needs and wishes of the locality," invest it with adequate power and assign to it appropriate finances, we will never be able to evoke local interest and excite local initiative in the field of development.

The proposals of the Planning Commission for the Second Five Year Plan, as accepted by the Parliament, stressed the need for creating within the district a well organized democratic structure of administration in which the village panchayat will be organically linked with popular organisations at a higher level. In such a structure the functions of the popular body would include the entire general administration and development of the area, other than such functions as law and order, administration of justice and certain functions pertaining to the revenue administration. We have now to examine whether the existing local bodies can take over and perform these functions and, if not, what new bodies should be created and with what jurisdiction powers and resources.

The district boards might have served the purpose for which they were created, i.e. educating our people in self-government; but they have neither the tradition nor resources to take up this work. They have also been handicapped by having too large a charge to receive their detailed attention. The chairman and members of the district board are not in a position to give any considerable portion of their time to the affairs of such a vast area. The very size of its charge compels delegation of a very large area of authority and discretion to its own officers, so that the effect is to replace State officers drawn from larger cadres by officers of limited experience in restricted fields. The tendency has been for the State to take over many of the functions of the district boards; even so, there is a sort of overlapping diarchy prevailing in certain aspects of administration. For instance, in one State, rural medical assistance is the function both of the Government and the district boards; the district board dispensaries are poorly equipped, poorly staffed and almost ineffective. The maintenance of most of the roads has been taken over by the State Governments. Nor will it be easy, convenient or practicable to link the village panchayat directly to the district board. In many States a district consists literally of hundreds of village panchayats and even in those where the village panchayats are large in jurisdiction, their number is inconveniently large. Under these circumstances the link between the district board and its constituent village panchayats cannot be a live one.

Primary education in many States has been assigned to the jurisdiction of district school boards, which, again, are bodies with inelastic revenues collected by others, so that financially they are mainly dependent on the Government and, therefore, can display very little initiative. The block advisory committees are generally nominated and never invested with the powers of decision even though their recommendations are generally accepted. We have found that often they are unrepresentative of some important sections of the local public. The district planning committee is, perhaps, even less powerful.

With this background, we have to consider whether the time has not arrived to replace all these bodies by a single representative and vigorous democratic institution to take charge of all aspects of development work in the rural areas. Such a body, if created, has to be statutory, elective, and comprehensive in its duties and functions, equipped with necessary executive machinery and in possession of adequate resources. It must not be cramped by too much control by the Government or Government agencies. It must have the power to make mistakes and to learn by making mistakes, but it must also receive guidance which will help it to avoid making mistakes. In the ultimate analysis, it must be an instrument of expression of the local people's will in regard to the local development.

This body can function effectively only if it is the sole authority for all those development programmes which are of exclusive interest for the area. In such matters the State government will cease to operate within the area and in special circumstances when it has to, it has to do so through the agency of this local body.

We do not consider this body necessary, merely because the present arrangements are not democratic nor because we think that we should 'give democracy to intermediate levels'. It is not theory or dogma which is impelling us to make these recommendations but practical considerations. Democracy has to function through certain executive machinery but the democratic government operating over large areas through its executive machinery cannot adequately appreciate local needs and circumstances. It is, therefore, necessary that there should be devolution of power and a decentralization of machinery and that such power be exercised and such machinery controlled and directed by popular representatives of the local area.

It is not infrequently that delegation of power is mistaken for decentralization. The former does not divest the Government of the ultimate responsibility for the actions of the authority to whom the power is delegated; this authority is under the control of the Government and is in every way subordinate to it. Decentralization, on the other hand, is a process whereby the Government divests itself completely of certain duties and responsibilities and devolves them on to some other authority. It is true that devolution of responsibility cannot be completed without a complete devolution of all the control over the necessary resources and admittedly such devolution cannot be completely feasible in any country. What we can work up to is to decentralize certain sources of income assured under statute and recommended that further resources should be made available by mutual agreement between the government and the local body. Delegation of powers is taking place to progressively lower levels of executive machinery. Decentralisation of responsibility and power, on the other hand, has not taken place below the State level in recent years. Such decentralisation has now become urgent and can be effected by a devolution of powers to a body, which, when created, will have the entire charge of all development work within its jurisdiction. The term 'development work' covers agriculture, animal husbandry, cooperation, minor irrigation works, village industries, primary education, local communications, sanitation, health and medical relief, local amenities and similar subjects. If this body is to function with any vigour, initiative and success, the Government will have to devolve upon it all of its own functions in these fields within the body's jurisdiction, reserving to itself the functions of guidance, supervision and higher planning—and where necessary, providing extra finance.

Fears have been expressed to us by many persons with whom we have discussed the scheme—officials as well as non-officials. These fears revolve round two points—inefficiency and corruption. We have been told, and we do not deny, that such a devolution of powers and responsibilities and the consequent decentralisation of the executive machinery may result in a fall in efficiency. Centralisation and even autocracy often appear more efficient than decentralisation and democracy. This may be true over short spans of time, but in the long run, we believe that democracy and decentralization assert themselves and succeed better especially in the field of local development and local welfare. Rural development and rural welfare are possible only with local initiative and local discretion. If, therefore, there is a fall in efficiency, as a consequence of such devolution and decentralization, such a fall will, we have no doubt, be temporary. The lack of efficiency of many of our present rural self-governing bodies has been due to too large a jurisdiction, too few powers and too scanty finances accompanied by absence of close relationship with the village panchayats and of wise guidance by Government or by political parties. Nor have any efforts been made either by the Governments or by public or political organizations to impart any training in administrative matters to persons elected to such bodies. We hope that our recommendations will remedy these defects.

The case of corruption is more complex. Its causes are numerous—there is the 'ignorance of the people which drives them through the fear of the machinery to pay its minions; there is the dilution of responsibility through various stages of delegation of powers unassociated with local opinion; and there is the constant possibility of the emergence of privileged groups—power tends to concentrate in a few hands and remain there. All these, however, are not phenomena new to this country or unknown in democratically governed foreign countries. They can be eliminated only by constant and intelligent vigilance on the part of the citizens. This, in the circumstances of our country, is possible only if the electorate knows at least by name the persons in whose hands they have placed power.

The jurisdiction of the proposed local body should be neither so large as to defeat the very purpose for which it is created nor so small as to militate against efficiency and economy. Obviously, the village panchayat is too small in area, population and financial resources to carry out all these functions. Obviously too, the next higher body will have to function through the panchayats as far as possible, for the very reasons for which such a body will be created. The various alternatives which we have considered are that this institution should be identical in extent with the N.E.S. Block, the tehsil or taluka, the sub-division (when this consists of more than one tehsil), or the district. Many districts are at present too large in area and/or population. And 'people', particularly in our circumstances cannot be expected to take a personal interest in and to make a personal sacrifice for common institutions at the local government level, unless these are small enough for their comprehension and are near enough for their influence to be demonstrably apparent.

The block, on the other hand, offers an area large enough for functions, which the village panchayat cannot perform and yet small enough to attract the interest and service of the residents. Additional some of the blocks are already functioning as the developmental units and have been equipped for this purpose with adequate personnel in different fields. It is true that there will have to be effective coordination at a higher level, perhaps the district level but we are of the view that the most efficient and useful arrangement in this regard is to have an elected self-governing institution whose jurisdiction would be co-extensive with a development block. Elsewhere in this report we have recommended that generally a block should not have more than 20 circles, each of which should cover a population normally not exceeding 4,000. Variations would naturally arise with the density of population, the nature of terrain, the system of communication, etc. Even within the same region blocks may differ in size and population. It is not unlikely that often the block can by slight adjustment be made to coincide with one of the existing administrative units like tehsil, taluka or thana, the primary consideration being that the block does not become unwieldy either in size or in population.

We have considered other alternatives such as boards at the tehsil level and sub-division level. The intention, however, is to devolve power and responsibility on to a local body for the purpose of carrying out developmental activities in rural areas for which purpose the block has been specially brought into being. The block advisory committee will be replaced by a statutorily powerful instrument of the local people's will, which can ensure that the expenditure of resources upon local works conforms with the wishes and the needs of the locality. Nor will this involve any increase in the overheads, as is feared by many, because the existing governmental machinery would continue to operate but under the control of this local authority; higher technical advice will be available from the district staff in position now. Some have expressed the fear that a block area may not be able to find competent persons in adequate numbers to function as chairman and members of this block authority. We do not share these fears; the country has found competent persons to take charge of its affairs at other levels; the needs and circumstances of the block level body will discover adequate personnel within its area.

The Taxation Enquiry Commission have observed that in most of the States a village panchayat, within its own jurisdiction, over laps higher bodies functionally as well as financially. They have suggested that the functions, finances and taxation powers of the higher body should be coordinated with those of the village panchayat, whose growth and efficiency will be one of the functions of this higher body to safeguard.

We feel that this would be secured by prescribing that this body which we tentatively propose to refer to as the panchayat samiti should be constituted by indirect elections from the village panchayats. The panchayats within the block area can be grouped together in convenient units, which can be Gram Sewaks' circles, and the panches of all the panchayats in each of these units shall elect from amongst themselves a person or persons to be a member or members of the panchayat samiti. We consider that such elected representatives should be about 20 in number in each panchayat samiti. These elected representatives will co-opt two women who are interested to work among women and children. Wherever the population of Scheduled Castes exceeds 5 per cent of the total population of the panchayat samiti area, one person belonging to a Scheduled Caste shall be co-opted; and similarly, one member of a Scheduled Tribe. In Scheduled Areas suitable safeguards should be provided to ensure that the tribal population is adequately represented. Where members of these groups have already been elected to the panchayat samiti in prescribed numbers, no co-option will be required. In addition, the panchayat samiti may co-opt two locally resident persons, whose experience in administration, public life or rural development would be of benefit to the samiti.

We have noticed that most of the smaller municipalities, especially those with populations of less than 10,000 are substantially rural in character. Their municipal constitution, however, deprives them of that administrative contact with the surrounding rural areas which we consider essential for the development of both. We, therefore, recommend that each of such municipalities which lie as enclaves within the jurisdiction of a block should be entitled to elect from amongst its own members one person as a member of the panchayat samiti. We would also suggest that, wherever possible, State Governments may convert such predominantly rural municipalities into panchayats.

It has been urged in many quarters that where the extent and importance of the local cooperative organizations justify, a number of seats equal to 10 per cent of the number of elected seats be filled by representatives of directors of the cooperatives functioning within the block. This can be done either by co-option or by election by the directors of all these cooperatives. We commend this suggestion. No other interest will be represented on the panchayat samiti, either ex-officio or by special provision for election, nomination or co-option.

We suggest that, wherever possible, it should be arranged that the panchayat samiti should have a life of 5 years and should come into being sometime in the third year of the Five Year Plan period. The samiti, once elected, will be able to see to the execution of the second-half of the Five Year Plan drawn up by its predecessor, draw up its own plan for the next period and shoulder the responsibility of seeing it through the first-half of the period. This would be in the interest of wise planning and efficient execution of the Plan.

The urgency for decentralisation is the greatest in the field of development and it is here that we consider that the panchayat samiti should begin to operate with the least possible delay. Its function should cover the development of agriculture in all its aspects, including the selection of the seed, its procurement and distribution, the improvement of agricultural practices, provision of local agricultural finance with the assistance of the Government and of the cooperative banks, minor irrigation works, the improvement of cattle, sheep, goats and poultry, the promotion of local industries, the supply of drinking water, public health and sanitation, medical relief, relief of distress caused by floods, earthquakes, scarcity, etc., arrangements in connection with local pilgrimages and festivals, construction and repair of roads which are of local importance (other than village panchayat roads), management and administrative control of primary schools, the fixation of wages under the Minimum Wages Act for non-industrial labour, the welfare of backward classes and the collection and maintenance of statistics. In those States where district boards or janapada sabha have undertaken the management of high schools these can be transferred to the panchayat samiti concerned. In addition, it will act as the agent of the State Government in executing any special schemes of development or other activities in which the State Government might like to delegate its powers to this local authority. We would strongly urge that, except where the panchayat samiti is not in a position to function in any particular matter, the State Government should not undertake any of these or other development functions in the block area.

We do not refuse to contemplate the possibility of charging this body with certain other functions, such as the maintenance and development of small forests, the responsibility for the maintenance of watch and ward establishment, excise and such other items. We feel, however that the immediate objective is to ensure that the development of the countryside is carried out as rapidly and efficiently as possible and through democratic processes. Only after the Governments are satisfied that these bodies are functioning as efficient democratic institutions, should they consider the transference to them of some or all of these extra duties and responsibilities together with the appropriate financial resources.

As we have already observed, one of the most important reasons for the comparative lack of success of our non-urban local self-governing bodies is their exceedingly limited and inelastic resources. As we contemplate that almost the entire development work of rural areas will be the charge of the panchayat samiti, we recommend that the following sources of income be assigned to them:

a) A statutorily prescribed percentage of land revenue collected within the block area in the anti-penultimate year; where this arrangement is likely to cause a very substantial disparity in the incomes of the panchayat samitis, the alternative is to divide equally between all of them a portion of the State's land revenue; we suggest that in either of these cases the land revenue assigned to the panchayat samiti and the village panchayat should not be less than 40 per cent of the State's net land revenue;
b) Such cess on land revenue, water rate for certain minor irrigation work, etc. as is leviable under the various Acts but excluding special cesses like sugarcane cess; we suggest that a minimum rate of cess should be prescribed by statute but the panchayat samiti should be encouraged to recommend the levying of a cess at a higher rate, so that this could be considered a local taxation measure;
c) Tax on professions, trades, callings and employment; we would recommend that this should be levied not by the village panchayat nor by the small municipality but by the panchayat samiti itself;

d) Surcharge on duty on the transfer of immovable property;
e) Rents and profits accruing from property, e.g., ferries, fisheries, etc., within its jurisdiction, where these ferries lie across roads constructed and maintained by panchayat samitis;
f) The net proceeds of tolls and leases on roads and bridges, etc., in the panchayat samitis;
g) Pilgrim tax;
h) Tax on entertainments, including amusements;
i) Primary education cess;
j) Proceeds from periodical fairs and markets, bazars, hats and shandies other than those held more frequently than once a month whether located on private land or otherwise;
k) A share of the motor vehicles tax;
l) Voluntary public contributions;
m) Grants made by government.

In the case of some of these taxes it will be necessary to prescribe a compulsory minimum rate. To make the panchayat samitis demonstrably useful to the village community and to ensure their continued success, it is necessary that the State Government should give them adequate grants-in-aid; some of these grants will be unconditional, others earmarked for certain purposes but without further conditions, some others earmarked for certain purposes but on a matching basis. The result will be that each panchayat samiti will have an assured income of a certain size and will attract grants-in-aid from Government by producing its own fresh resources. In making these grants the State Government will, no doubt, take into account the special economic backwardness of certain areas and give them appropriately larger grants.

At present State Government spend money on rural development mainly through their own machinery and small amounts through village panchayats; but public funds are also spent in another manner i.e. by direct assistance to what are known as non-official bodies which are all non-statutory. Certain central organizations which spend public funds on specified aspects of rural development, function either through their own branch organization or through these non-official bodies. We recommend that all Central and State funds spend in a block area should invariably be assigned to the panchayat samiti to be spent by it directly or indirectly, except to an institution, assistance to which is either beyond the panchayat samiti's functions or its financial resource.

The panchyat samiti will have two sets of officers, i.e. those at the block level and those at the village level. The former will include the chief officer the executive officer and various technical officers in charge of agriculture, roads and buildings, irrigation, public health, veterinary, cooperation, social education, primary education etc; the chief officer will be statutorily vested with administrative powers subject, of course, to necessary checks. These powers will be somewhat similar to those of the chief executive officer or commissioner of a municipality. We would here quote and emphasise the recommendation of the Committee of Local Bodies which was made at the 1954 Conference of the Local Self-Government Ministers—

> "For improving the standards of administration in local bodies there is a very good case for separating as far as possible, their purely executive functions from their deliberative or policy making functions. The latter category of functions should appropriately be the sphere of the elected wing of the local bodies. Once policies and decisions have been adopted, however, their implementation and execution should be left to the principal executive officer who must be made primarily and directly responsible for this part of the work. As a necessary corollary to this principle, the more important executive posts in the local bodies should be centralized on a State-wise basis and should be made transferable".

All of these officers will be drawn from the corresponding State cadres and will be lent to the panchayat samiti by the State Government, which will meet the cost of their pay, dearness allowance and pension and leave contributions; the panchayat samiti will meet the expenditure on the current allowances, like travelling allowance, which will be at rates prescribed by the State Government. These officers will be transferable by the State Government or by the heads of departments. According to the current practice the village level employees like the Gram Sewak, the primary school teacher, etc., will be recruited by the zila parishad who will assign them to the various panchayat samitis, the terms of their service being prescribed by the State Government. They will be under the administrative and operational control of the chief or executive officer.

The panchayat samiti will need guidance in technical as well as administrative matters; but this guidance should, under no circumstance, result in excessive regulation or control; nor should such guidance or advice be considered as interference. With this object we suggest that the technical control of the corresponding district level officers be under the administrative and operational control of the chief administrative officer. The annual budget of the samiti will, in our opinion, have to be approved by a higher and more experienced body on which Government also will have to be represented. At the same time we do not believe that a local self-governing body can display any initiative and vigour, if its budget has to be scrutinized and approved in all details by a Government functioning from a long distance or its officers in the district. We, therefore, suggest that the budget of the samiti will have to be approved by the zilla parishad.

A certain amount of control will inevitably have to be retained by the Government, e.g. the power of superseding a panchyat samiti in public interest. It may also be necessary that the collector should be vested with certain powers to suspend a resolution of a panchayat samiti when he apprehends a breach of the peace or where the action proposed to be taken by the panchayat samiti is ultra vires of the Constitution or contrary to the law of the land.

The panchayat samiti will have an elected chairman. But during the first two years after its creation the panchayat samiti may have the sub-divisional officer, parent officer or revenue divisional officer as the chairman. This suggestion is made merely to ensure that the administrative machinery of the block is assembled and set in motion by a person with administrative experience.

Together with the establishment of the panchayat samiti, we consider it necessary to prescribe its relations with the village panchayat and to redefine the functions and resources of the latter. Apart from the organic link between the village panchayat and the panchayat samiti, it is necessary that a similar connection should exist between the Gram Sewak and the village panchayat. This can be secured by making him the development secretary of the Gram Panchayat, or, if there are more panchayats than one, of a committee of the village panchayats within the jurisdiction of each Gram Sewak. This committee, composed of the sarpanches and upsarpanches of each of the village panchayats, should coordinate the budgets and formulate and execute the plans of all the village panchayats in the circle. Of this circle committee the Gram Sewak should be the development secretary. He will thus ensure that his own activities and the programmes of the various village panchayats are in complete consonance.

In regard to the constitution of the panchayat, we suggest that this should be purely on an elective basis, but that there may be a provision for the cooption of two women members and one member each from the Scheduled Castes and Scheduled Tribes in conditions similar to those prescribed for the panchayat samiti. We do not consider that members of any other special group need any special representation either by election or cooption.

These panchayats will have as their main resources:

a) Property or house tax as is considered locally suitable;
b) Tax on daily, bi-weekly or weekly markets, bazars, hats or shandies, whether located on private land or otherwise;
c) Tax on carriages, carts, bicycles, rickshaws, boats and pact animals;
d) Octroi or terminal tax;
e) Conservancy tax;
f) Water rate;
g) Lighting rate;
h) Income from cattle-ponds;
i) Fees to be charged for registration of animals sold within the local area, for the use of sarais, slaughter house etc.
j) Grants from the panchayat samiti on lines similar to those suggested for grants from Government to panchayat samiti.

In the case of some of these taxes it will be necessary to prescribe a compulsory minimum rate.

As far as possible, the village panchayat should be used as the agency for the collection of land revenue; this arrangement has been tried and found successful in some States. It may be necessary to grade the panchayats on the basis of their performance in the administrative and developmental field. For instance, the rates at which it is imposing taxation, the success with which it collects its taxes and the extent to which it displays active interest in developmental activities would be the criteria on which such grading is based. Only those village panchayats which satisfy a certain basic minimum of efficiency will be invested with the power of collecting land revenue. In all cases, however, such power will be restricted to amicable collection as distinct from the collection through processes of law. One of its main advantages is that the panchayat's other income is supplemented by the commission for collection. In addition, we recommend that the village panchayat should be entitled to receive from the panchayat samiti a statutorily prescribed share of the net land revenue assigned to the latter as per our suggestion in an earlier paragraph. We suggest that such share may go up to three-quarters.

The resources of the village panchayats are necessarily inelastic and every effort should be made to assist them to add to them. We have noticed that, a certain States, villagers have to pay for their watch and ward. This arrangement differs not merely from what prevails in other States but also from the obligation of urban citizens in the same State. As long ago as 1881, urban municipal bodies and, therefore, the urban citizens were relieved of the responsibility for local watch and ward; the municipalities were then instructed that the resources till then used on expenditure for watch and ward should thereafter be diverted towards the extension of educational facilities. We, therefore, suggest that the local resources which the village panchayats now raise and spend on the maintenance of watch and ward staff should, in future, be used for development purposes.

We have noticed, as have many others, that the collection of panchayat taxes is generally not satisfactory. Arrears accumulate until they are merely written off; and it is not always that the assessee fails to pay because of his inability to do so. We, therefore, suggest that legislation should provide that a person who has not paid his taxes in the penultimate year should be debarred from exercising his franchise in the next panchayat election and that a panchayat member should automatically cease to be such, if his tax is in arrears for more than six months.

The budget of the village panchayat will be subject to scrutiny and approval of the panchayat samiti; and the panchayat samiti will provide such guidance to the village panchayat in all its activities as the latter may need. The chief officer of the panchayat samiti will exercise the same powers in regard to the village panchayat as the Collector and District Magistrate will exercise in regard to the panchayat samiti. On the other hand, no village panchayat should, be superceded except by the State Government, who will, however, do so only on the recommendation of the zila parishad.

We find that statutes in different States have imposed different duties on the panchayats; the Saurashtra Law entrusts them with 182 specific duties, while the Bombay Act gives a list of 16 compulsory and 21 discretionary functions. The Taxation Enquiry Commission was of the opinion that it would be wise to assign to the panchayat a few well-chosen and clearly defined duties and that these should be coordinated with similar functions assigned to higher local bodies; on the other hand, the Local Self-Government Ministers' Conference 1954 held the contrary view.

As we contemplate that the village panchayat will receive substantial grants from the panchayat samiti and that its budget should be approved by the latter, it would be a workable arrangement to prescribe a smaller number of compulsory functions and permit the panchayat to undertake any other developmental work with the approval of the panchayat samiti—such approval being automatic with the approval of the budget. We, therefore, recommend that the compulsory duties of village panchayat should be: (i) provision of water supply for domestic use, (ii) sanitation, (iii) maintenance of public streets, drains, tanks etc., (iv) lighting of the village streets, (v) land management, (vi)maintenance of records relating to cattle, (vii) relief of distress, (viii) maintenance of panchayat roads, culverts, bridges, drains, etc., (ix) supervision of primary schools, (x) welfare of backward classes and (xi) collection and maintenance of statistics; in addition, it will act as the agent of the panchayat samiti in executing any schemes of development or other activities—some of the subjects find a place in the duties assigned to the panchayat samiti, but the provision that the village panchayat budget has to be approved by the panchayat samiti will guard against any duplication.

The constitution of the panchayat samiti and the arrangements mentioned above should ensure the maximum amount of cooperation and coordination between the village panchayats and the panchayat samitis.

One of the banes of democratic village administration in some areas has been the intensification of factions and feuds, often also of separatism arising out of caste distinctions. The system of electoral contests at village level has often added to these. The committee to report on the problems of reorganization appointed by the Planning Commission's Panel on Land Reforms considered this particular problem and observed that "Efforts should be made to ensure that elections to the village panchayat are made, as far as possible, by the general consent of the people and the bitterness and hostility created by election campaigns is avoided. The membership of the village panchayat should be regarded as an opportunity for service to the people which should be undertaken by the best men in the village rather than as a means of obtaining power and prestige. At the same time, it is necessary to bear in mind the dangers which are inherent in unanimity, arrived at under pressure. Such unanimity may actually, over a period, develop below the ground conflicts which could have worse effects than the usually passing conflicts in an open election." But we are genuinely concerned about this aspect of village public life and apprehend that unless a suitable and effective solution is found, it will spell ruin to all schemes for community development. What is required is a complete freedom to exercise the right of adult franchise without the possibility of creating tensions, which aggravate village feuds and caste differences. We are not able to suggest any arrangement, which could secure this.

Though we are primarily concerned with organizations for rural development, we would like to make a reference to the judicial powers of the panchayats. In many States village panchayats are invested with certain judicial powers, both criminal and civil. There is, however, a feeling that they can not exercise them freely within the limited area under their jurisdiction, without inviting the wrath of the party which loses the civil suit or the criminal case. We would, therefore, recommend that judicial panchayats may have a much larger jurisdiction than even a Gram Sewak's circle, possibly, two or three such circles. The village panchayats concerned may suggest panels of names and, from out of these panels, the sub-divisional magistrate or the district magistrate may select persons who will form the judicial panchayat.

We have already indicated the reasons why in the matter of developmental activities village panchayats and the panchayat samitis should be the main local bodies. Having assigned to them functions in various fields, we feel that there is very little left for any higher administrative executive body other than the Government. The district board, the district school board and the janapada sabha become superfluous, as local interest, supervision and care, necessary to ensure that the expenditure of money upon local objects conforms with the wishes and needs of the locality, are provided by the panchayat samiti, which we consider a body of size adequate in population and area. The functions which these bodies are at present performing will, in our opinion, be performed with greater efficiency by the panchayat samiti. To ensure the necessary coordination between the panchayat samitis, we suggest a zila parishad of which the members will be the presidents of the panchayat samitis, all members of the State Legislature and of the Parliament representing a part or whole of a district whose constituencies lie within the district and district level officers of the medical, public health, agriculture, veterinary, engineering, education, backward classes welfare, public works and other development departments. The Collector will be the chairman of this parishad and one of his officers will be the secretary.

Some of the functions of the parishad have already been indicated; for instance, it will examine and approve the budgets of the panchayat samitis. Where funds are allotted by the Government of the district as a whole their distribution between the various blocks will be made by the and consolidate the block plans, annual as grants for special purposes are needed or demand samitis, these also will be consolidated and forwarded agreement by the parishad. It will also generally supervise of the panchayat samiti. It will also replace the present District Planning Committees.

It may be necessary to have standing committees of the zila parishad to ensure rapid disposal of work. In particular, a standing committee for finance, consisting of the chairman and two non official members and another for service matters, consisting of the chairman, a non-official member and the district level officer of the department concerned with any particular case, would be not merely useful but necessary. Also considerable delegation of powers will be necessary in the matter of approving the budgets of the panchayat samiti, so that where there is no reason to suggest modifications, the approval can be rapidly conveyed.

We do not contemplate that this parishad will have executive functions; that way lies danger to the initiative and, therefore the effectiveness of the panchayat samitis in their early years. Nor do we consider that the district level officers on the panchayat samitis should be members of the parishad without the power to vote; that would be the surest insurance for indifference. The time is long past when we could think of the officers' interest in rural development as something different from or contrary to that of the non-official.

It has been suggested that these indirect elections may lead to party politics of a bitter nature percolating from the district headquarters to the panchayat samiti and through them to the village panchayat causing bitter electoral contests and ruining the peace of the villages so essential for a cooperative efforts towards community development. We are not impressed by this argument. Nor do we see how direct elections, either to the panchayat samiti or to the zila parishad, can guard against the danger of active politics withering the chances of community development.

The creation of the panchayat samiti and the zila parishad and the devolution upon them of the responsibility of supervising, guiding and assisting the village panchayat and the panchayat samiti, respectively, obviate the need for continuing the maintenance of a separate directorate of panchayats with its own departmental officers for control and inspection. Whatever supervision, guidance and assistance, are necessary, will be provided by higher bodies in the constitution of which the lower bodies will have a dominant voice. And only the zila parishad will in all matters directly with the Government or Commissioner or Divisional Officer where such functionaries exist.

It is possible on the basis of the experience of the working of this panchayat samiti that we may decide to decentralize the administration further; possibly, it may be necessary to alter the composition, scope and powers of the zila parishad. Again, there is little doubt that after a few years the powers vested in the Collector and District Magistrate may fall into desuetude and may be statutorily withdrawn.

It is also possible that some of the State Governments may find it useful to devolve upon the zila parishads in a progressively larger measure the powers now exercised by them directly through their district level officers. In such a case the zila parishad will have to be a purely elective body with, perhaps, a few co-opted members. These phases are difficult to forecast and, therefore, a blueprint of developments in the direction of further decentralization would be difficult and profitless to attempt.

In the ultimate analysis, the establishment of the panchayat samitis with a wide devolution of powers by the State Government has to be an act of faith—faith in democracy. But, as we have mentioned, some of the persons whom we examined, both officials and non-officials have expressed doubts about the success of what they have called 'an experiment in democratization'. These doubts, if shared by the State Government, may at best, justify a phasing of the process of the creation of the panchayat samitis. If a State Government is inclined to such a view, we would recommend that they should take a district as a whole and extend the Act to all parts of it at the same time; it is only when the three tiers of our scheme, viz. the village panchayat, the panchayat samiti and the zila parishad operate simultaneously, will we get the maximum out of it.

We have already observed that no efforts so far have been made either by the Government or by public or political organizations to impart any training in administrative matters to persons elected to local bodies. Such training is essential if we are to make out local bodies effective and useful. Rural administration (especially its developmental aspect) is an increasingly complex process and its machinery is also growing more complex. We have suggested various schemes for integration of the different parts of such machinery but, even so, it will continue to be complicated. It has to be handled with care, and that care can come either from a certain volume of initial knowledge or from knowledge born out of a series of mistakes. To provide the former and avoid the latter, it is necessary that the persons elected to or aspiring to be elected to such bodies should be equipped with a certain minimum knowledge of this machinery. Organization of 'summer schools' for this purpose will have to be seriously considered both by the State Governments and by responsible non-official organizations like State associations of panchayat samitis.

These recommendations give an overall picture of the machinery which we consider essential for democratic decentralization and which alone can lead to effective rural development. Some of the State Governments have, however, expressed the view that in the circumstances obtaining in their States they consider it advisable and convenient to devolve power on to a local body whose jurisdiction is as large as a district. While we are convinced that devolution of power to a smaller body would be the most effective method of democratic decentralization, we do not refuse to visualize similar devolution to a district body, instead. Such a district body will have to be fully empowered by statute, to carry out all developmental activities in the district in the same manner as we have recommended for the panchayat samiti, though on correspondingly a larger scale. The appropriate funds and powers of taxation, on the lines suggested by us in an earlier paragraph for the panchayat samiti, should be available to this district body as also the requisite field staff and the supervisory staff at district head-quarters. In the blocks selected for intensive development work under the C.D. programme, a panchayat samiti will have to be constituted on the lines similar to what we have already proposed. This samiti will carry out the community development programme; we recommend that they will also carry out (as agents of the district body) all other developmental activities proposed for that area by the district body. All funds – the district funds as well as funds for intensive development will, in the first instance, be at the disposal of the district body which will transfer them to the panchayat samitis concerned in the community development areas. All activities, which can be performed by the panchayat samiti, should normally be assigned to it. Only in areas where there is no community development programme sanctioned may the district body operate directly. The district body will generally concern itself with inter-block and district level activities and institutions. The district body, which we have referred to above, will inevitably have to be constituted on a purely elective basis. We suggest that members of the village panchayats, within each panchayat samiti area in the district, should from amongst themselves, elect a prescribed number of persons and these should form the district body; care will, of course, be taken to ensure that this body is not too large to be effective as an instrument for rural development. Similar arrangements could also be worked out if it is found feasible or convenient or desirable to devolve power to a body which will have a sub-division of the district for its jurisdiction.

Development can not progress without responsibility and power. Community development can be real only when the community understands its problems, realizes its responsibilities, exercises the necessary powers through its chosen representatives and maintains a constant and intelligent vigilance on local administration. With this objective, we recommend an early establishment of statutory elective local bodies and devolution to them of the necessary resources, power and authority.

II. Ashok Mehta Committee: 1978

PANCHAYATI RAJ: REVIEW AND EVALUATION

India has gathered wide experience in the practice of democratic decentralization in the wake of the recommendations of Balvantrai Mehta Study Team. The extent and form of democratic decentralization have varied from State to State and there have been ups and downs in the earnestness with which the programme has been pursued. The task of reviewing and assessing developments over the past decade and half is greatly facilitated by the valuable evaluations made by Expert Committees appointed by different State Governments and the Government of India from time to time. A voluminous literature has grown upon the subject. It would, therefore, not be necessary to cover the ground again. We need confine ourselves to the main lessons the past experience has to teach and draw upon them for the future of Panchayati Raj.

With the dawn of freedom, thought had to be given to the method of involving people in their own welfare in a democratic state. Adult franchise spread the participation of the people in the selection of their representatives in the legislatures of the States and the Parliament of India. This by itself was not sufficient for the attack on the basic problems of a welfare State. As a first step, States started renewing the old concept of Gram Panchayats and Gram Sabhas through legislations, so that people's involvement in their affairs at the grassroots can be started. This approach was reflected in the First Plan document which referred to the need of "establishing over a period of years panchayats for villages or groups of villages". They visualized civic and economic activities for a village community as one of the functions of panchayats. This concept was added on by Community Development Programmes started in 1952. Along with this concept it was felt necessary to build up an administrative system which can tackle the welfare problems of growth at the local level. The National Extension Service followed Community Development as the vehicle through which idea of Community Development will be worked. The Service was constituted at the block level with a network of Village Level Workers. The public participation at the block level was through nominated representatives of the public. As experience of this new approach grew, a feeling also developed that probably the public involvement was not representative enough and as such not effective. This was reflected in the Second Plan document where there was reference to the necessity for speeding up the development of democratic institutions within a district. They invited attention to enhance responsibilities of the district administration. This came in the wake of an attempt to disaggregate the State plans into district plans. It was therefore, reiterated that "unless there is a comprehensive village planning which takes into account the needs of the entire community, weaker sections like tenant-cultivators, landless workers and artisans may not benefit sufficiently from assistance provided by the government". The Plan visualized democratic structure of administration within the district in which village panchayats would be organically linked with popular organizations at higher levels.

The Balvantrai Mehta Study Team was appointed in January 1957 to study and report on the Community Development Projects and National Extension Service with a view "to economy and efficiency" and, among others, "for the assessment of the extent to which the movement has succeeded in utilizing local initiatives and in creating institutions to ensure continuity in the process of improving economic and social conditions in rural areas". The Community Development Projects and National Extension Service envisaged the necessary inputs, coordinated action and provision of staff on the developmental side. They also sought additional changes. A schematic budget for the comprehensive development of the block was made available by the Government of India; it was also to be made operative, at the block level, with the help of nominated advisory committees. The National Extension Service created for the first time a development entity separate from the revenue administration. It was this institutional framework which was to be considered by the Balvantrai Mehta team.

The Balvantrai Mehta Team offered two broad directional thrusts— first, it argued that there should be administrative decentralization for the effective implementation of the development programme and that the decentralized administrative system should be under the control of elected bodies. As the authors of the report would put it, "Development cannot progress without responsibility and power. Community development can be real only when the community understands its problems, realizes its responsibilities, exercises the necessary powers through its chosen representatives and maintains a constant and intelligent vigilance on local administration. With this objective we recommended an early establishment of statutory elective local bodies and devolution to them of the necessary resources, power and authority". This, according to the report, was the meaning of democratic decentralization in operational terms. Secondly, the basic unit of democratic decentralization should be located at the block/samiti level. They contemplated just an advisory role for the district tier.

The National Development Council, "affirmed the objective in introducing democratic institutions at the district and block levels and suggested that each State should work out the structure which suited its conditions best. "Thereafter, based on the broad suggestions of the Balvantrai Mehta Study Team most of the country was covered with Panchayati Raj Institutions in the succeeding decade. The total number of Gram Panchayats covered 90 per cent of the rural population. 4,974 blocks had 4,033 samitis, since some had opted for districts and talukas as the key unit. Out of 399 districts, 262 Zilla Parishads were also conceived with varying degrees of actual power.

A bird's eye view of how Panchayati Raj Institutions have fared in some States would provide valuable insights into the structural and operational aspects of Panchayati Raj. It may be stated as a general provision that in a country of India's size and diversity, certain unevenness in performance is inevitable. Historical vicissitudes further complicate the picture. Structures and functions have been changing over the years. In Assam there have been shifts in the tiers and functions assigned; the prevalent ones are the Mohkuma Parishad at the sub-divisional level and the Panchayat with a population of well over 15,000. In Andhra Pradesh, the Zilla Parishads, endowed with limited executive functions have shown encouraging results in areas like education; the performance of Panchayat Samitis too has been noticeable. In Bihar, the Zilla Parishads were introduced only in 8 districts, but were soon given up. In Rajasthan, which, with Andhra Pradesh, was the first to introduce Panchayati Raj, the Samiti tier worked with enthusiasm in the initial phase. Tamil Nadu and Karnataka do not have the Zilla Parishad, in the sense of a body endowed with executive functions; but the samitis/Taluka Boards they have done well. The performance of the Samitis in Tamil Nadu, in regard to education, water supply, roads and nutrition, has received wide appreciation. In Kerala, where there were only Village Panchayats but some of a size which could amount to half a block, the working has been extremely satisfactory in the field of many municipal and civic functions; it is worth noting that, in spite of different political parties being represented on the elected body, there was the needed harmony in implementing the programmes assigned to them as also in monitoring certain developmental projects. In Uttar Pradesh, a large number of small panchayats were set up together with Zilla Parishads with very limited powers. They could not achieve much owing to extreme paucity of powers and resources. In Madhya Pradesh, the Act embodying the scheme of democratic decentralization was sought to be implemented in a piec-meal manner – an approach that proved counter-productive. As far as West Bengal is concerned, it has weaned away from what seemingly was a four-tiered structure to a three-tiered one with larger gram panchayats. Deviating from the Balvantrai Mehta Report, a three tier structure with the first point of decentralisation at the district level was organized in Maharashtra and Gujarat and it has functioned effectively, particularly in the field of decentralized planning and development. The District Councils in North Eastern India have features which are worth studying.

The story of Panchayati Raj has been a story of ups and downs. It seems to have passed through three phases—the phase of ascendancy (1959-64); the phase of stagnation (1965-69); and the phase of decline (1969-77).

A number of developments in the past have conspired to undermine the Panchayati Raj structures and made them ineffective. In fact, except in Maharashtra and Gujarat, the PRIs have been rarely given an opportunity to take up planning or implementational work on a sizeable scale. Broadly speaking, the miniscule programmes which were assigned to village panchayats or the few items of work which were part and parcel of the Community Development Programme were handed over to the newly elected Panchayati Raj Institutions. The essential idea that all developmental activities should flow only through the block level organization lost ground, though Panchayat Samiti as a key unit of decentralisation was, in most cases coterminous with the block. In practice, there was a movement in the opposite direction. Scheme like Small Farmers Development Agency (SFDA) or Drought Prone Areas Programme (DPAP) or Intensive Tribal Development Project (ITDP) were not brought within the purview of the elected Zilla Parishads either in Gujarat or in Maharashtra. The staff under the Zilla Parishad would execute the schemes though the programmes were kept outside their orbit. Again, in Maharashtra, the planning work was entrusted to a body outside the Zilla Parishad under the chairmanship of a Minister. Further, in the process of implementation of the transferred activities, here and elsewhere, a number of orders and directions by the State Government led to the gradual development of subsidiary legislation which would tend to curtail the decision making powers of the elected bodies. The staff spread by the State to the district and lower bodies also gradually came to consist of officers who were not wanted by the State Governments. There was also the phenomenon of the tapering off of the Plan allocation resources contributing to as also symbolizing the decline of Panchayati Raj. Finally, the quantum of own resources contemplated for the panchayats were both meager and their potential also was not exploited by the Panchayati Raj Institutions in good measure.

Will for strengthening the PRIs further weakened with the demands of developmental programmes being kept out of its orbit becoming stronger. The tempo of development administration in seed supplies, fertilizers distribution, promotion of minor irrigation or enforcement of the civil supplies regulations, procurement of foodgrains, or performance of other welfare functions required such an intensive effort the year round that all the available staff at lower levels had almost to be requisitioned back by the parent departments. It is the vastness and growing complexity of developmental programmes that has sometimes been used as an excuse for by-passing the PRIs in the name of their structural inadequacies without PRIs being entrusted with these challenging tasks.

Role of bureaucracy: Bureaucracy had probably its own role in dissociating the PRIs from the development process. Several factors seem to have conditioned their perception. The system of line-hierarchy would find favour with them as an organizational principle. The officers would feel that they are primarily accountable for results and financial proprieties to the State Government. The officials knew no better than to trust their own fraternity. They would, on the one hand, therefore, be averse to PRIs being entrusted with additional functions and on the other would not easily get adjusted to working under the supervision of elected representatives. The new developmental tasks and their load also became such that the bureaucracy had to commandeer all the available staff and, in the process withdrew what was available for the block. Further, as a natural corollary of this pull for withdrawal, the influence of the field bureaucracy in decision-making waned with time and that of secretariat or departmental heads increased. The field bureaucracy was further handicapped because the elected representatives also quite often failed to own and work with them.

Political Will Weakens: In sum, an overview of the national scene would indicate that the activities of PRIs were meager, their resource base weak and the overall attention given to them niggardly. The functioning of the Panchayati Raj System thus became discouraging. As if this was not enough, some of the State Governments would postpone the holding of elections or supersede some of important tiers of PRIs for one reason or the other. The lukewarm attitude of the political elite at higher levels towards strengthening of the democratic process at the grassroots was generally the crux of the matter. Of particular significance in this connection is the relative cooling off of enthusiasm of MPs and MLAs in some States towards Panchayati Raj, because they would perceive a threat in emerging Panchayati Raj leadership to their position in their respective constituencies. In the ultimate analysis, all this led to a weakening of political support to PRIs and of the administrative will to work through them.

Lack of conceptual clarity: Worst of all, there was lack of clarity in regard to the concept of Panchayati Raj itself and the objectives for which it should stand. Some would treat it just as an administrative agency; others as an extension of democracy at the grass-roots level; and still others as a charter of rural local government. What is all the more intriguing is the fact that all these conceptual images would co-exist side by side tending to militate against each other at least in the short run. None of them could perhaps be seriously pursued. This led to a crisis of expectations all along the line.

Ways of disillusionment on Structural: In general, there has been disappointment with the working of PRIs which is traced, in stronger or milder terms, to a number of inadequacies and failure, PRIs are dominated by economically or socially privileged sections of society and have as such facilitated the emergence of oligarchic forces yielding no benefits to weaker sections. The performance of PRIs has also been vitiated by political factionalism, rendering developmental trusts either warped or diluted. Corruption, inefficiency, scant regard for procedures, political interference in day-to-day administration, parochial localities, motivated actions, power concentration instead of service consciousness – all these have seriously limited the utility of Panchayati Raj for the average villager. It has also been argued that planning and implementation being a matter of expertise, require quick as well as complex arrangements of details and as such the inter-position of Panchayati Raj bodies has on the one hand adversely affected the pace of development administration and on the other has further complicated the problems of coordination.

SOUNDNESS OF THE SYSTEM

Such a pessimistic appraisal is not shared by all. The basic soundness of the system, with necessary correctives, is strongly emphasized by many. They feel that the dominance of oligarchic elements is a malaise affecting the political system and vitiating the implementation of development programmes at other levels also. The democratization process as a component of modernization, should tend to destablise traditional leadership in the long run. There could however, be no shortcut to this process and as such no easy way to remove the influence of the entrenched groups except by referring the issue at regular intervals to the larger electorate. This is, however, not enough, unless a series of measures and provisions to protect the weaker groups and strengthen their active participation are taken. However, PRIs alone could not be picked up for blame in regard to the neglect of the interests of the weaker sections, as even the Government of India did not seem to have followed the lead in favour of weaker sections, recommended in 1961 by the Jayaprakash Narayan Committee till 1970 when it was revived with the slogan 'Growth with Social Justice'. It has also been argued that an excessive concern for factionalism and party politics often betrays an inadequate appreciation of the dynamics of competitive politics in a democratic society. It has been further brought out that the problems of corruption and inefficiency are embedded in the social complex and no level of polity is immune from them. The same is true of procedural irregularities. Similarly, general factors like social milieu, situational compulsions, context of scarcity, mal-adjustment with a fast changing environment, inadequate knowledge and the like are wide spread and affect officials as much as they do the non-officials and that also at all levels of the polity. Altogether thus, Panchayati Raj should not be singled out for criticisms, failure and pitfalls which are not peculiar to it alone.

It would, in fact, be wrong to conclude from the existing evidence that PRIs have failed in the sphere of planning and development. It is true that PRIs cannot be a substitute for physical and human inputs. For example, in agricultural development, irrigation facilities, consolidation of holdings, regulated markets, net-work of cooperatives, development of communication system and, above all, a peasantry proud of agriculture as a profession are the inputs for which PRIs in no way can be treated as a substitute. The story of development of the Punjab and Haryana would clearly bring this out. But it is equally true that given the inputs, if PRIs are involved in the developmental process, planning will be realistic, programming will cater to the felt needs and priorities of the people and implementation would evoke people's involvement and participation. The fact of the matter is that PRIs have not been given a chance to serve as a vanguard of development in village India. Wherever they have been given the responsibility to whatever limited extent, as in Maharashtra and Gujarat, they have done well.

GAINS OF DECENTRALIZED DEMOCRACY

Summing up, we can say that it will be wrong to think that Panchayati Raj should be viewed as a god that has failed. It has many achievements to its credit, the more important of which may be identified here. Politically speaking, it became a process of democratic seed-drilling in the Indian soil, making an average citizen more conscious of his rights than before. Administratively speaking, it bridged the gulf between the bureaucratic elite and the people. Socio-culturally speaking, it generated a new leadership which was not merely relatively young in age but also modernistic and pro-social change in outlook. Finally, looked at from the development angle, it helped rural people cultivate a development psyche.

APPROACH AND RECOMMENDATIONS

We are departing from the conventional mode of presenting our views, suggestions and recommendations in the form of an itemized summary because our main endeavour throughout has been to lay down a new approach towards the Panchayati Raj Institutions—not in the usual point by point way but rather in concentrically circles, as they interact and depend on one another. The formulation of structures, functions and the utilization financial, administrative and human resources of Panchayati Raj Institutions should, in our opinion, be determined on the emerging functional necessity of management of rural development. In our Report, we have attached importance to the direction rather than specific on certain items usually done and hitherto highlighted in various cognate Reports. The institutional, structural and functional specifics of Panchayati Raj would, in our opinion, vary over time as well as space; we can do no more than indicate the spectrum of possibilities while the various State Governments would have to work out the actual details keeping in view their changing requirements. Whatever be the variations, they have to be round the crucial theme of linking institutions of democratic decentralisation with socially motivated economic development.

In this approach, it is not necessary to dwell too long on the past, except to locate the trend and draw guidance for the future. The dis-association of the growing and complex programme of development with Panchayati Raj Institutions which were considered inadequate, the inability of the bureaucracy to be attuned to execute the programme through elected bodies, the lack of political will to foster these institutions, several internal deficiencies in the functioning of Panchayati Raj Institutions and above all, the lack of clarity about the concept itself have weakened the entire system.

Part of the disappointment arises from the syndrome that they have not been assigned significant functions and tried continuously and with zest. The developmental programmes were not channeled through them. Some of the comments like the emergence of oligarchic tendencies are inherent in the social milieu, and some others are common to other tiers of the polity also. Panchayati Raj

Institutions should not be singled out for these comments. It has many achievements to its credit in introducing a process of democratic seed drilling in the Indian soil, in breaking the gulf between the bureaucratic elite and the people and in generating a new leadership not merely relatively young in age but pro-social change in outlook.

Panchayati Raj, like democracy at the national and State levels, is both an end and a means. As an end, it is an inevitable extension of democracy; as a means, it would continue to be responsible for discharging obligations entrusted to it by the national and State Governments in sphere not yet transferred to its exclusive jurisdiction. Altogether, both as an end and a means, Panchayati Raj should contribute to the philosophy as well as practice of a rich, rewarding life in rural India.

The establishment of democratic bodies below the State level is an imperative from the political and socio-developmental perspectives. Democratic institutions with periodic elections at all levels will provide a forum for the assertion of their strength in large number by the weaker sections. With the people and political parties having adequate opportunities to exercise power at various levels, national energy in political recrimination will yield to constructive competition and mutual co-operation in developmental activities among political parties.

Our recommendation to transfer substantial quantum of powers from the State Government to the local bodies, is bound to have concern with the existing scheme of distribution of powers between the Union and the State, which would require a detailed but separate consideration. In order to achieve requisite status as well as continued functioning, the Committee agree that some provision in the Constitution deserves a careful consideration of the Government of India.

On account of growth of the span, spatial scatter and the complexities of the development activities, as also significant changes in the strategies, the context of institution building in rural India has undergone a change since the submission of the Report of Balvantrai Mehta Study Team in 1957.

Among the striking changes in rural India, the most important have been (a) imparting of dynamism to agriculture which was previously stagnant (b) the enlargement of the concept of agriculture to cover allied occupations like dairy, piggery, fishery, social forestry, etc. which are of special relevance for the economy of the weaker sections (c) assured availability, on an increasing scale, of new agricultural technology including scientific utilization of major and minor irrigation (d) emerging shifts in national policies towards cottage, village and rural industries at localized production points (e) increasing possibilities for absorption of institutional credit for effective implementation of productive projects (f) growing importance of marketing, involving a series of extra local transactions (g) the emergence of growth centres and need for tackling the rural urban continuum (h) increasing emphasis on group action and conjoint activities (i) growing concentration on special efforts to organize and assist the weaker farmers in particular and poorer sections of society in general, and finally (j) coupled with the developmental urges, the evolving need for provision of the welfare and municipal utilities requiring, in the rural areas, different types of technical servicing functions.

The institutional, structural and functional contours of Panchayati Raj have to be in conformity not only with the accelerating pace of development but also with its strategies and policies. New structures of development administration or local level development management will have to be taken into account the functional necessities of the on-going development thrust. Panchayati Raj Institutions in the coming decades should, therefore, be equipped to undertake democratic development management under conditions of rapid changes, continuous growth and sustained innovations in all spheres of rural life.

State Governments should realize the social costs of administering expanding development programmes from a distance or through only governmental machinery. When they delegate the responsibilities for implementation to lower levels, they can concentrate on refinement of strategies and higher-level policy making in the management of challenges of development administration in areas such as rural land structural deficiencies, agricultural modernization, rural industrialization, credit universalisation and planning for fuller utilization of natural resources.

STRUCTURES, COMPOSITION AND ELECTION

The Institutional Design for Panchayati Raj should take into account the functional necessity of propelling the on-going developmental thrusts, built upon the intricacies at the appropriate levels and transmit the impulse to the people through location-specific involvement.

The emerging scenario of the dynamics of development necessitates that the technical expertise of a high order be made available at levels below the State to sustain the momentum of rural development, which in many cases, has been already administratively decentralized at the district level. The inescapable compulsion, therefore, is that the district should be the first point of decentralization, under population supervision, below the State level.

Below the district level, the balance between technological requirements and possibilities for meaningful participation by the people in development management can, in our view, be best achieved, by grouping a number of villages to constitute Mandal Panchayats. These would not only ensure an economic viability; thus will enable the people's representatives to exercise democratic supervision over the large number of micro-projects which are to be implemented at the local levels in the coming years. Most of these projects are not entirely village based but would require a span of technology beyond the capacity of a Village Panchayat. The attention to the family based programme, often covering as many as four hundred families, needs larger unit to tackle them than at present. Such a Mandal Panchayat would cover a population of 15,000 to 20,000 and would also facilitate the forging of necessary linkages with schemes for development of focal points and growth centres and would ensure efficient management of the growing rural-urban linkages.

While our preference is for two tiers—a district level Zilla Parishad and Mandal panchayat—we are conscious of the fact that two other tiers are already in existence and it may take time for the suggested institutional design to take shape and become fully operational. The block-level Panchayat Samitis, where they exist now, would be converted into non-statutory executive committees of Zilla Parishads and when the Mandal Panchayats become active, most of their functions would be taken up by the Mandal Panchayats. As a transitional structure, the Block can, therefore, continue as per the convenience of the State keeping in view their requirements and the stage of development. At the village level, the people would be involved in Mandal Panchayats through Village Committees which would look after the municipal functions and related welfare activities. Till the Mandal Panchayats are constituted, a federation of existing Village Panchayats may be desirable.

Regarding the composition of the various tiers of Panchayati Raj, we would like to suggest only a broad pattern. We would, however, like to make it clear that whatever be the structural arrangements, the directly elected element must preponderate over the others at all levels. In the elections, the Scheduled Castes and Scheduled Tribes should get representation on the basis of their population. The Chairman of Zilla Parishad will be elected indirectly. The President of the Mandal Panchayat may, however, be elected directly or indirectly as the States may decide. The term of all the elected tiers should be 4 years, and, as far as possible, election to all these bodies should be held simultaneously.

Our proposals regarding the structures would have to be necessarily modified in case of areas with pre-dominant tribal population or in hilly or desert areas. Thus, in tribal areas Mandal Panchayats may be formed for smaller population as necessary. Again in tehsils/blocks where strong traditional tribal organizations are functioning, they may be allowed to look after their social functions. Similarly, structures established by the Constitution under Scheduled VI need not be disturbed.

The Zilla Parishad should consist of six types of members, viz. members elected from suitably demarcated electoral divisions, Presidents of the Panchayat Samitis on an ex-officio basis, nominees of bigger municipalities, nominee of district level cooperative federation, two women who have secured the highest number of votes in the Zilla Parishad elections (in the event of no women coming forward for election, two women may be co-opted) and two co-opted members, one with special interest in rural development and the other drawn from University/College teachers. The Chairman of the Zilla Parishad would be elected from amongst the directly elected and ex-officio members by all the members.

The Zilla Parishad would function through a number of Committees, the more important ones being constituted for Agriculture, Education, Small Industries, Finance and Public Works. The composition of all the Committees would be on the basis of proportional representation so as to ensure representation to all sections and shades of opinion. A Committee of the Chairman of these Committees will function as the Standing Committee on Social Justice in Zilla Parishad as well as at other levels also.

All members of the Zilla Parishad and M.L.A.s, M.L.Cs and M.Ps from the concerned district shall constitute the Planning Committee at the district level for plan formulation and periodic review.

A suitable Committee for dealing with the problems of Education staff like transfers to be comprised of members of Zilla Parishad, a representative of the State Government and the District Education Officer with a view to bring in evenness and method in transfers and postings.

Panchayat Samitis, till they continue to exist, should consist of the following categories of members—(1) Presidents of the Mandal Panchayats, where they have been constituted, on ex-officio basis, (2) Zilla Parishad members elected from electoral divisions in the Mandal Panchayat areas, (3) nominees of smaller municipalities and block-level cooperative federations, (4) one co-opted member, having special interest in rural development. The President of the Panchayat Samiti would be elected from amongst the ex-officio and directly elected members of the Zilla Parishad from the Samiti area by all the members. In approximately 1000 Talukas Blocks (where either the Scheduled Castes constitute 20 per cent of total population or the Scheduled Tribes are majority of population) the Chairmanship of Panchayat Samitis can be reserved for them.

The Mandal Panchayat would consist of the following categories of members:

a) 15 members directly elected on village-cum population basis;
b) representatives of Farmers' Service Societies;
c) two women securing the highest votes in Mandal Panchayat elections (if none contested, two women may be co-opted).

The President of the Mandal Panchayat would be elected by the directly elected members from amongst themselves. The President may however, be elected directly as the States may decide. Seats may be reserved for Scheduled Castes/Scheduled Tribes on a population basis in the Mandal Panchayat. A Committee with all women members of the Panchayat represented on it would also ensure that decisions are made by women themselves on priorities and choices in welfare and development programmes specifically for women and children.

The Village Committee would consist of the following categories of members—(1) members elected to Mandal Panchayat from the respective electoral unit, (2) members elected to the Zilla Parishad from the respective electoral units, (3) representatives of small and marginal farmers. The Village Committee will be presided over by the members of Mandal Panchayat elected from the village concerned.

The Gram Sabha has an important role in activating the democratic process at the grass-roots and deserves genuine encouragement. The proposed Village Committees would have the special obligation to organize two Gram Sabha meetings every year to explain to the people what programmes the Mandal Panchayats are executing in their area and to channelise the people's feed-back to the Mandal Panchayat.

The Nyaya Panchayats like the Gram Panchayats were adopted as institutions for dispensation of justice at the local rural level.
Even as the working of Nyaya Panchayat has shown mixed results, in most cases they remained inactive. The administration of justice on a decentralized basis has its merits but the functioning of the existing Nyaya Panchayats have not been able to elicit popular satisfaction.

The Committee are of the view that Nyaya Panchayats should be kept as separate bodies and should not be mixed with the people elected for development panchayats. The members of development panchayats wield executive powers and there are chances that justice may suffer if the two functions are combined.

The Committee are in favour of a combination of a qualified judge to preside over a bench of separately elected Nyaya Panches. The elected Nyaya Panches will not be entitled to seek re-election; they should serve in an area other than that from which they have been elected.

Panchayati Raj elections should be conducted by the Chief Election Officer of the State in consultation with the Chief Election Commissioner.

The State Government should not supersede the Panchayati Raj Institutions on partisan grounds and if supersession becomes necessary, these should be replaced by an elected body within six months. The State Governments should not postpone elections of Panchayati Raj Institutions.

Participation of political parties in Panchayati Raj elections would ensure clearer orientation towards development programme and facilitate healthier linkages with higher level political process. Direct elections coupled with programme based contests, would offer great scope to weaker sections for availing of the opportunities offered by the political system.

FUNCTIONS

The functions devolved upon Panchayati Raj Institutions being highly location-specific, exhaustive list of functions, in an all India perspective, will not have much operational relevance. Local priorities in all development programmes vary from region to region and it is, therefore, necessary that the States and the Union Territories should have adequate scope for evolving their own list of functional priorities.

Our basic approach with regard to decentralization is, that of spectrum of functions and tiers; development being a dynamic process, functions cannot remain static. Periodic adjustments would, therefore, have to be made in the functions devolved upon Panchayati Raj Institutions to suit the changing requirements. But this does not mean that decentralization can be viewed as a political charity or administrative concession. The functional agenda of Panchayati Raj Institutions would be inescapably determined by the unfolding logic of "dynamics of development" in the interests of effective implementation. State Governments would have no choice but to decentralize adequate powers and functions and provide proportionate financial resources at the relevant local levels.

Keeping in view the foregoing approach, all the development functions relating to a district which are now being discharged by the State Government would have to be placed under the Zilla Parishads. Some of the functions which can be so decentralized include—agriculture and allied sectors, health, education, communication, rural industries, marketing, welfare of backward classes, family welfare, etc. Even under these heads certain parts may have to be with the State Government. Thus, functions such as agricultural research college and university education, medium irrigation projects and other similar items involving complications or cutting across district boundaries may not be transferred to Zilla Parishads.

Under the new scheme envisaged by us, the decentralization would commence with the district as the first point and further movement below will take place depending upon the situation in each State. Broadly, the Zilla Parishad will handle all the decentralized State programmes and plan for them at the district. The Mandal Panchayat will handle the implementation work.

Mention is needed for co-operation (which should remain outside the purview of Panchayati Raj Institutions) and education (which must be entrusted to Panchayati Raj Institution). In our view, cooperation should not be under the Zilla Parishad as it would be placing one set of elected bodies under another. The Panchayati Raj Institutions can limit themselves to motivating and organizing the co-operative movement at this stage. As regards education, we feel that it can be transferred to Zilla Parishad with the proviso that a committee should be specifically constituted to look after transfers and postings. Supervisions by local bodies will, in our view, not only improve the attendance of teachers but it is anticipated that the ratio of drop-outs will decrease. The programmes on adult education will also be accelerated.

The entrustment of development functions to Panchayati Raj Institutions would remain incomplete unless all the Panchayati Raj Institutions are vested with the authority to take their own decisions and plan according to their own requirements. Planning would, therefore, be an important function to be discharged by the Zilla Parishads.

The functions of the Mandal Panchayats would have to be viewed from a new angle. They would be responsible for implementation of the schemes and projects assigned by the Zilla Parishad. These would be many. They would have to play a promotional role in activating community action, build up organization and project formulation. They would continue to perform the functions conventionally assigned to them under various statutes. They would have increasing role to play in the sphere of municipal and welfare functions.

Elaboration of an omnibus list of Mandal Panchayat functions has no relevance unless there is genuine decentralization accompanied by corresponding resources. The foregoing classification of the Mandal Panchayat functions would, indeed, facilitate the process of decentralization by helping the task of identification of areas in which further decentralization can take place. What is, therefore, needed at the Mandal Panchayat is purposive work allocation and transfer of money component along with the functions assigned to them for implementation. This would not only introduce clarity into the expenditure pattern, as also help the State-level Heads of Departments in specifying the operational procedures for execution of various plan projects. In general, Mandal Panchayats have to administer, co-ordinate and provide institutional supervision to on-going field level projects.

The Panchayati Raj Institutions in general and the Mandal Panchayat in particular can play an important role in the sphere of municipal and welfare functions by supplementing the State Plan outlays in this regard. Many of these requirements might be so local that even such comprehensive programmes as the R.M.N.P., may not be able to cover them; but the Mandal Panchayats are more intimately concerned about such items.

In view of the fast moving developments and transitions, the regulatory functions may continue to be vested in the Collector but such regulatory functions which are germane to implementation of various development programmes should be assigned to the appropriate tier of Panchayati Raj. Further, the Revenue Department should be reoriented to encourage and facilitate the working of Panchayati Raj Institutions.

The devolution of regulatory functions upon the Panchayati Raj Institutions may be reviewed in due course of time when the Zilla Parishads have been properly established and are in a position to make and implement their own plans with the quantum of resources available or placed at their disposal.

The Mandal Panchayats would have to be suitably integrated with growth centres. They would have to take the necessary decisions concerning marketing, inputs supplies credit and servicing and welfare requirements in association with other organizations in this regard.

In due course of time the Mandal Panchayats will have to be base level organization for project implementation and as such they would not only take over the functions of the Block but higher level technical expertise will be made available at lower levels. Some of the block level functions would have to be moved upwards as only the district level body would be competent to discharge them.

PLANNING

With the district as the strategic level for economic planning, the Zilla Parishad should be made responsible for planning at the district level. The appreciation of the total resources, the credit availability and the necessary strategy formulation covering several blocks would be feasible at the district level. An elected Zilla Parishad would also provide the much needed correctives to the techno-economic plans. The production and employment programmes prepared at the Block level will fit into the totality of the plan.

A professionally qualified team should be stationed at the district level for preparation of district plans. The composition of this group would be on the lines suggested by the Expert Group on Block level Planning. While formulating the plans, the expertise of the district level staff should take into account a cross section of all shades of public opinion relevant to the district.

The State Government would have to provide continued assistance in the process of district planning. It would have to ensure that the national objectives relating to weaker sections are pursued by the Panchayati Raj Institutions. They will also have to provide the financial and physical parameters as well as technical expertise to the technical group. It should also ensure equitable allocation of resources and fixation of long range priorities.

The district plan prepared by the technical group would be placed before the "Committee of the whole" of the Zilla Parishad where the MPs, MLAs and MLCs are also members.

The State Government should provide necessary machinery for examining the district plans to enable formulation of the State Plans. It should also hold a dialogue with the Zilla Parishads in this regard.

The District Planning should take care of urban-rural continuum. The District Plan should also analyses data on growth points and growth centres in order to provide for necessary economic flows.

Intensive exploitation of new opportunities of resources earmarked for the weaker sections should be a part of the plan process itself. The District Social Justice Committees will be of considerable help in this regard.

The on-going exercise of District Planning should also take into account the formulation of sound projects and short-term action plans covering areas of specific endowments, poverty belts and specific target groups.

In order to avoid the problem of non-implementation and non-absorption of the many "delivery system" which are already functioning, the several implementation components of all the local level projects should be analysed in advance and greater attention should be paid towards synchronization and orchestration of the activities of the project-level functionaries of the different disciplines. Coherent activity analysis, standardized micro-project plans including flowcharts of goods, services and functionaries will also have to be prepared so that the Mandal Panchayat can play an effective role in administrative coordination and institutional supervision.

At present some districts are too large to facilitate drawing up of composite plans. Keeping in view, among others, the guidelines of compactness, affectivity, manageability and the number of representatives in Zilla Parishad, smaller districts would be desirable.

To begin with, the Mandal Panchayats may be limited to implementation and promotional roles, but they would have a key role in supplying the necessary information about the various schemes and suggest the potential areas of development as well as their requirements to the Zilla Parishad. They would have to play this role on a continuing basis and not merely by holding a meeting to consider draft plan or sending their comments on it to the Zilla Parishad. The planning unit at the district level should take note of the views articulated by the Mandal Panchayats from time to time.

The total credit inflow for agricultural development is expected to rise significantly in the years to come. The Panchayati Raj Institutions should, therefore, pay greater attention to the institutional finance rather than concentrating on budgetary sources as in the past. This would be possible only if the Panchayati Raj Institution pay due attention to ensuring greater responsiveness in project implementation by ascertaining the views of the beneficiaries since these require considerable people's participation like the Revised Minimum Needs Programme.

The Panchayati Raj Institution should not only be regarded as a forum for obtaining the views of people's representatives but in due course, they should become capable of planning for themselves within the resources available to them.

WEAKER SECTIONS

The Scheduled Castes and the Scheduled Tribes constitute the bulk of the rural poor and their welfare has been enjoined by the Directive Principles of State Policy. Besides a number of development programmes have been launched for this purpose. The inability as well as the structural inadequacies of the Panchayati Raj Institutions to benefit the weaker section of society have made us very anxious to provide structural as well as programmatic remedies to ensure that they derive, in adequate measure, the benefits of the planned development of the country. Their confidence in the developmental role of Panchayati Raj Institutions and participation in the functioning should be assured through several measures.

Among the institutional device for ensuring adequate representation commensurate with their numbers we would like to recommend the following—(i) in order to provide a fair deal to Scheduled Castes and Scheduled Tribes their representation in all Panchayati Raj Institution should be on the basis of their population, (ii) 666 talukas/blocks where the Scheduled Castes constitute more than 20 per cent of the population and in 329 talukas/blocks where Scheduled Tribes constitute a majority of population, the principle of reservation should be extended to elective offices, (iii) the reservation system can be supplemented by formulation of Social Justice Committee where the Chairman should be only from Scheduled Castes/Scheduled Tribes, (iv) with a view to provide political support to the objective of protection of the interests of the weaker section's Committee of the Legislature with, as far as possible, majority representation of MLAs/MLCs belonging to Scheduled Castes/Scheduled Tribes should be set up to review the working of the programmes meant for these communities. This Committee would also be responsible for Social Audit of funds earmarked for Scheduled Castes/Scheduled Tribes.

In order to ensure that the weaker sections of society derive maximum benefits from the various plans we would like to suggest that there should be an independent authority to carry out 'Social Audit' of the funds and programmes earmarked for the Scheduled Castes and Scheduled Tribes and ensure that projects designed for them are implemented in a way that the desired impact is not diluted. To begin with, a separate wing may be created in existing audit set up and Collector may be made responsible for supplying to the Government all the data required for Social Audit.

Development programmes leading to diversification of the occupational pattern have a great degree of relevance for the Scheduled Castes and Scheduled Tribes; the Panchayati Raj Institution should be involved in opening up these occupational vistas in rural areas in such fields as dairying, poultry farming, piggery, fisheries, scrub jungle forestry, etc.

Panchayati Raj Institutions as people's institutions can provide the field level support to Finance/Development Corporations for Scheduled Castes/Scheduled Tribes, (which are in operation in some States and should be established where not yet in existence) providing financial and technical assistance for various programmes beamed at Scheduled Castes and Scheduled Tribes.

It should be the special responsibility of the State Government to ensure, through purposeful administrative measures (both protective as well as developmental), that the scale-neutrality of the new technology is maintained, credit flow is made accessible to the poorer sections of society for credit-worthy programmes and development of their skills is continuously fostered. A number of physical resources are still available under the control of Panchayats and Panchayat Samitis which are not being fully realized for the benefit of the poorer sections of the community. In some cases certain influential people in the village have encroached upon such resources. The State Governments should undertake necessary eviction proceedings and launch a vigorous drive to restore these to the Panchayati Raj Institutions; it is also necessary that the relevant regulatory functions should be placed under Panchayati Raj Institutions as part of their developmental functions.

Among the various development programmes which can be implemented for the benefit of weaker sections on the hitherto unused or neglected communal resources we would like to make a special mention of social and far forestry and brackish water piscine culture. Composite culture of brackish water fish and prawns has an immense economic potential which must be harnessed for the benefit of the weaker sections. The scientific utilization of unused areas under forests and protected forests as well as the areas lying between villages and reserve forests where various easement rights prevail can be used to settle landless labour as well as provide effective support to animal husbandry. A time-bound programme to link up the development of such land and water resources with the poorer families should be made an important part of States' responsibility to be implemented through Panchayati Raj Institutions and continuously monitored by the Social Audit Agencies, the Social Justice Committee and the Committee of Legislature.

ADMINISTRATION

Our basic approach to remoundling of the administrative organization of Panchayati Raj Institutions is that administration must drape well with the body politic and fit its contours. With the decentralization of the functions of the State Government, all the concerned district-level officials would, therefore, have to be placed under the Zilla Parishads and lower tiers. A separate development administration functioning on a decentralised basis would, thus, develop along with a composite Zilla Parishad Secretariat.

The constitution of elective organization to supervise and direct development programmes would certainly upset the existing administrative routines but the various problems of personnel management and personal adjustments should not be allowed to stand in the way of this change over, the administrative apparatus would have to adapt itself to this fundamental change.

The Maharashtra and Gujarat experience provides many pointers to tackle the problems relating to promotions, protection of pay and other emoluments and maintaining uniformity in service conditions. Generally speaking, all staff of Gazetted rank in Class I and Class II should continue to remain on the cadres of the State Government while the Class III and Class IV should be fully handed over to the Panchayati Raj Institutions. There should be adequate provision for inter-changeability between the State level officers and Class I and Class II working under the Zilla Parishads. The recruitment of the Zilla Parishad staff may be done by independent State and district-level boards.

All development staff with the Zilla Parishad should be placed under an officer to be designated as the Chief Executive Officer of Zilla Parishad. The Chief Executive Officer will achieve horizontal coordination vis-a vis the other district heads who will be Secretaries of the respective subject committees of the Zilla Parishad with Chief Executive Officer being an invitee to the Committees' sittings.

Zilla Parishad will be responsible for policy formulation supported by any specific decisions taken by its committees, but the main responsibility for the entire implementation work should be that of the Chief Executive Office. The Development executive should be of a sufficiently high rank; a person who has successfully "done" a district for a period of not less than 3 years should, therefore, be appointed as Chief Executive Officer.

Some transitional, mainly personnel problems involved in division and transfer of the entire district staff into State and District cadres are inevitable.

Even after the decentralisation of district level functions to Panchayati Raj Institutions, the State Government would continue to maintain some district level staff for the execution of its schemes but the extent of dualism of staff would be restricted to State functions which would be determined at the time of decentralizing the powers to the Zilla Parishad.

The collector would continue to exercise the regulatory, revenue and other functions assigned by the State Government. He would also organize and help the conduct of 'Social Audit'. The role of the Collector may have to be reviewed later when some of the regulatory functions of the State are sought to be transferred to the Zilla Parishad.

Mandal Panchayat would be handling the developmental as also municipal and welfare functions. It would, therefore, be possible for them to have a full-time Panchayat Executive Officer, instead of part-time assistant. His salary and emoluments should be appropriate to attract sufficiently qualified personnel. There is considerable staff of different development departments at the field level—in due course, this staff (e.g. such officials as the Agricultural Extension Officer, the Veterinary Stockmen, the Fisheries Extensions Assistant, Commercial Crop Extension Workers, Small Industries Promotion staff and the Health Sub-centre staff etc.) should move to the Mandal Panchayat level.

As far as technical inputs are concerned, the line-hierarchy will not be broken. The staff in the Zilla Parishad will be under the control of their superiors for technical matters giving scope for technical line control but they would be under the Chief Executive Officer for purpose of administrative control. The Confidential Character Rolls of the District level technical staff written by the Chief Executive Officer will, therefore, be countersigned by the concerned Head of Department. The Confidential Character Rolls of the Chief Executive Officer, written by the Chairman, could be countersigned by the Commissioner of the Division.

On account of increase in the volume of development work and their growing complexity, it would be necessary to constantly study the developmental requirements and mould the structure and functions of the State-level departments looking after the Panchayati Raj Institutions. There should be a Minister for Panchayati Raj whose main tasks would be as follows:

a) Enactment of Panchayati Raj legislation;
b) Elections to Panchayati Raj Institution;
c) Training of elected office bearers and executive officers and administration of all Training Centres meant for the Panchayati Raj system as a whole;
d) Promotion of Audit of Panchayati Raj Accounts;
e) Review of Panchayati Raj activities for report to the State Legislature;
f) Promotion of camp training of elected members of Panchayati Raj.

For the routine administrative work, a strengthened Directorate of Panchayati Raj and a Secretariat Department under a Development Commissioner would be necessary but all the development departments would have to play a role in the successful working of Panchayati Raj Institution.

As a part of the evolution of a new administrative culture, the Heads of Departments from the State Headquarters can call on Chairman, Zilla Parishad on their visits to the districts to acquaint him with the essential features of the visit. The Chairman, Zilla Parishad should also establish rapport with the various State level Directors for achieving smoother and streamlined delivery systems.

The Panchayati Raj statutes should be so framed as to facilitate the transfer of full powers. The responsibility of the Council of Ministers at the State level is particularly significant in this regard as two Committees of Legislature will be looking after the entire performance of Panchayati Raj Institution.

The State Government should also arrange for periodical independent evaluation of the working of Panchayati Raj Institution by independent agencies including educational institutions with the universities playing an important part.

The Government of India also have the special obligation to strengthen the process of democratic development management at the rural level. They have to ensure that development programme falling in the district sector do not, in any way, by-pass the Panchayati Raj Institution. The suggestions made by us such as increasing the training facilities will require the Centre to play a positive role.

FINANCIAL RESOURCES

The current situation in the flow of funds to Panchayati Raj Institutions from diverse channels has been analysed and the possibilities have been pointed out for either strengthening or emulating the procedures from other states, for augmenting the resource. While this process may have to continue for sometime, it requires to be emphasized that any proposals for financial devolution or financial decentralization should not emanate from a traditional approach but from our basic commitment to the logical imperatives of the dynamics of development which clearly postulate the entrustment of a great deal of developmental functions at the district level, with the Mandal Panchayat playing a key implementation role.

Apart from the budgetary devolution from the State Government, the Panchayati Raj Institutions also should mobilize enough resources of their own. No democratic institution can continue to maintain its operational vitality by depending upon external resources. The thesis "no taxation, only representation" should be discouraged. For this purpose, all Panchayati Raj Institutions should have compulsory powers of taxation. A select list of taxation powers should be given to the Panchayati Raj Institutions and out of them some should be made compulsory. It is not possible to have a standard list for all States. But certain taxes like house tax, profession tax, entertainment tax, special taxes on 'land and buildings' should be levied compulsorily by the Panchayati Raj Institutions at appropriate level.

The taxation powers given to the Panchayati Raj Institutions should be limited and specific and must not operate iniquitously. Certain occupations and professions in which the weaker sections predominate should be exempted through statutory provisions, in order to ensure social justice.

Incentives can be offered for optional taxes realized. These may take the shape of award of prizes or provision of matching grants.

In addition to taxes, the Panchayati Raj Institutions should levy fees/taxes for services like lighting, sanitation, water supply, etc. The maxima and minima of these fees should be laid down to avoid arbitrariness or lack of uniformity.

At this stage, land revenue, cess on land revenue, cess on water rate, surcharge on stamp duty, entertainment tax and show tax etc, should also be assigned to the Panchayati Raj Institutions with higher percentage to Mandal Panchayats. To provide local initiative, the Panchayati Raj Institutions must be statutorily empowered to request the State Government to increase the cesses. In this context, the Committee recommend the complete transfer of land revenue to Panchayati Raj Institutions in a phased manner over a period of five years taking into account the buoyancy of other taxes.

In the emerging rural development programme, the transfer of public properties such as porambokes, grazing lands, unreserved forests, orchards, public lands, cattle ponds, fishery tanks, ferries, quarries, etc. would have great significance and these should be statutorily vested in the Mandal Panchayat in the cases where it is not already done.

This is not a mechanical transfer but for the purposes of maximizing the yield out of these resources; this activity will increase as a part of their functions. In the emerging context of escalation in their potentialities and fiscal worth, markets, hats, shandies, fairs etc. will be a significant source of revenue. Hence, custody of such fairs, hats and other markets should be vested with the Panchayati Raj Institutions.

With a sizeable population base and a territorial jurisdiction covering a number of "markets" the Mandal Panchayat would be able to tap a more diversified resource-base with greater intensity and elasticity. It is these revenue yielding sources that should be built up both with budgetary support of Government and institutional finances. Such sources will be mostly with Mandal Panchayats but can be transferred to Zilla Parishad, depending upon the size of the source. A scheme of support by State Government from budgetary sources carrying small or no interest supplemented by institutional finance would go a long way in helping the Panchayati Raj Institutions to proceed with their aims of establishing remunerative enterprises.

Apart from the taxation powers of their own and transfers effected through several possibilities indicated earlier, a permanent annual grant of not less than Rs. 2.50 per capita should be available to the Mandal Panchayats. It should be the objective; the quantum of several transfers should be, at least, to this target.

As the power to impose taxes should not be divorced from the responsibility for their collection, the officials of the Panchayati Raj Institutions should themselves collect the taxes.

Combination of Patwari and Secretary as per the suggestion of the Santhanam Team is not desirable. At the time of consolidation of holdings, the provision for reserving areas for common purposes should be strictly enforced and these should be entrusted to the Mandal Panchayats. It would be possible for the Mandal Panchayat to be economic on too many part time or full time low paid Secretaries and get the services of a better paid Secretary who would look after the collection of taxes and also be responsible for the other functions entrusted to the Mandal Panchayats.

The burden of collection of land revenue should be left optional to the concerned Panchayats, but the Mandal Panchayats collecting land revenue should get a commission commensurate with the results so as to provide a built-in incentive. When the Mandal Panchayat comes into full-fledged existence the policy may, however, be reviewed again.

When all functions relating to Plan implementation at district level are transferred to the Zilla Parishad, this will also involve transfer of the finance along with projects. The allocation of the projects/ Plan funds has to be done on a formula worked out to achieve equity among the Districts and weightage to backward areas. Further, the non-plan expenditure incurred at the district or lower levels should also be under the administration of the respective tiers, since it would be conducive for composite development work and build up the capabilities of Panchayati Raj Institutions.

Administrative expenditure on the salaries, allowances, etc. of the staff transferred as on the date of transfer, be given as a grant to the Zilla Parishads or to the other concerned tiers.

The appointment of a State Finance Commission does not appear to meet the situation. The major thrust is more on achieving an equitable distribution of plan allocations.

The establishment of a new financing body, like a Panchayati Raj Finance Corporation, dependent partly on public borrowing, is not likely to add to the total availability of the credit. What is required in this context is a greater rural orientation to all the financial institutions to facilitate greater flow of credit to rural areas.

The pattern of budgeting, followed by the Panchayati Raj Institutions, should be simple.

The State Governments also will have to evolve a budgetary

procedure which will indicate the transfers of different types to the Panchayati Raj Institutions.

Each State Government may, taking into account the local circumstances, prepare comprehensive guidelines for the use of their officers and Panchayati Raj Institutions for preparation as well as for approval of budgets.

An important element to be emphasized both in the preparation of the budget as also in its format is the emphasis need to be placed on sufficient allocation and earmarking of the funds for the projects for the weaker section. The quantum provided and the appropriate utilization for the target-groups would be within the jurisdiction of the Social Audit.

Approval of budget by a higher authority seems to be a desirable practice, as it provides a linkage and also enables the higher level tiers of Panchayati Raj to know what is happening at the lower tiers and also to make suggestions for better utilization of such funds.

A sufficiently high ranking finance officer should be placed at the district level as the entire plan and non-plan funds would be under his supervision.

Every State should endeavour to present consolidated finance accounts of Panchayati Raj Institutions to the Legislature.

State Governments should immediately review the delay in audit which is partly caused by inadequate staff and partly by lackadaisical procedures.

Quick clearance of the outstanding audit objections pertaining to Panchayati Raj Institutions has special importance in view of the proximity and involvement of people's representatives with the expenditure at these grass-root levels.

A concurrent audit by the Examiner of Local Funds Accounts should be made operative instead of post audit.

Procedures for submission of utilization certificates by the Panchayati Raj Institutions for the grants given by Government must be made simpler.

The State Governments should consider the establishment of a Committee of the Legislature to be specifically concerned in the financial and physical performance of Panchayati Raj bodies. Along with the consolidated finance accounts, the State Government should also lay on the table of the Legislature, an administrative report on Panchayati Raj Institutions.

HUMAN RESOURCES DEVELOPMENT

The human factor is not only a component of growth but also shapes the texture of the society. In many ways, therefore, the human resource is more vital than the financial. Development of human resources should be, therefore, a primary feature of Panchayati Raj Institutions.

There should be three types of training—(i) for officials, (ii) for elected representatives and (iii) combined course for both officials and elected representatives together. The programme content would vary as suited for each participating group.

The training programmes, covering officials as well as non-officials, would be of a staggering dimension. This would require not only the activation of the existing institutions but also considerable augmentation of their numbers and resources. Suitable remedial measures should also be taken to resuscitate and revitalize the State-level training institutions.

The National Institute of Rural Development should be the apex all India institution for training of trainers, field studies, developing consultancy capabilities, research work and improvement in the level of training in the States. Its faculty should be strengthened and upgraded for this purpose. The Government of India has an important role to play in this regard.

There should be an evaluation for each of the training programmes so that it will be possible to make necessary modulations from time to time.

Importance should be attached to the programmes for adult education to develop the latent civic consciousness in all the people and thus strengthen the faith in the working of the Panchayati Raj Institutions. The Panchayati Raj Institutions should have a major role in organizing such programmes.

As a large segment contributing for the successful operation of a democratic system, special attention is to be paid to the role of women in Panchayati Raj Institutions. Their role could be strengthened in two ways—by allowing them to participate in the election processes more actively and also by giving them opportunities for decision making.

To secure their participation in elections for the two seats reserved for women in the Zilla Parishad and Mandal panchayat, any woman who gets the highest number of votes in the election even if she does not win, should be taken in as a co-opted member.

There should be a Committee of Women to operate and look after specific programmes which largely concern women and children. This would ensure that they do not become victims of the processes of change and that decisions are made by women themselves on priorities and choices involved in their programmes. Such a Committee should have the powers of the Mandal Panchayat with reference to the programmes specifically assigned to them.

In designing the Rural Industrialization programmes there should be special efforts to concentrate on programmes to provide gainful employment to rural women. This will also strengthen their management capabilities.

The formation of Mahila Mandals should be encouraged.

The present and the future success of the democratic process through Panchayati Raj Institutions lies with the rural youth.

Rural youth is not yet fully covered by the Yuvak Mandals; this weakness has to be attended to. Young farmers' clubs can be formed to activate the interest of the rural youth both in Panchayati Raj institutions and rural development.

The Yuvak Mandals should be given the status of an associate body in Panchayati Raj Institutions through suitable legislative measures.

Panchayati Raj Institutions have a motivational task in organizing Nehru Yuvak Kendras. It would be advantageous to organize National Service Scheme camps through the Panchayats.

The role of voluntary agencies in mobilizing people's support for Panchayati Raj will be crucial. They should be strengthened and encouraged to supplement the efforts of the Panchayati Raj Institutions. The motivational and promotional role of the Panchayati Raj Institutions should be clearly spelt to build up and facilitate the work of voluntary agencies and women's organizations.

Voluntary agencies with requisite expertise, proven standing and well-equipped organization can assist Panchayati Raj Institutions in the Planning process. They can be involved in formulation of projects and schemes and to create strong public opinion in support of measures aimed at social change.

RELATIONSHIP WITH OTHER INSTITUTIONS

Panchayati Raj Institutions are expected to take up the overall view of the economic and social well being of the people, while the co-operatives have to meet economic requirements. The relationship between Panchayati Raj Institutions and co-operatives has thus to be of coordinate rather than of a subordinate character.

The pattern of functional relationship between the Panchayati Raj Institutions and cooperatives will broadly be of five types:

i) Functions which could more appropriately and effectively be discharged by co-operative institutions.
ii) Functions requiring concurrent and conjoint action of Panchayati Raj and co-operative Institutions.
iii) Co-operatives functioning as agents of Panchayati Raj Institutions.
iv) Functions in respect of which co-operatives require facilities from the Panchayati Raj Institutions.
v) Where co-operatives participate in functions which are essentially the responsibility of Panchayati Raj Institutions.

Panchayati Raj Institutions should undertake the promotional and coordinational work like motivation and organization of co-operatives. The regulatory functions in respect of cooperatives should be done by the co-operatives themselves.

Representation from the co-operatives on the Panchayati Raj Institutions will be helpful in providing an institutional dialogue between the Panchayati Raj Institutions and the co-operatives. A reciprocity of representation of Panchayati Raj Institutions on the co-operatives does not appear to be necessary.

Urban-rural relationship is to be viewed in the context of needs of a developing economy and the attendant processes of affording higher levels of services and facilities. Integration of rural urban areas in a balanced reciprocity of economic and social growth can be achieved by linking up the rural areas with urban points.

With the existing small panchayats, in due course, giving place to larger Mandal Panchayats, the relationship between the Mandal Panchayats and small municipalities would become more purposive and meaningful; with some amount of equality, they can even enter into formal relationships for supplies and services.

The merger of small municipalities with Mandal Panchayats would be desirable. The focal points and growth centres will facilitate this process.

For purposes of composite planning the District Plan should encompass the development aspects of urban areas and the civic aspects of rural areas.

The representation of the municipalities in Zilla Parishad and other appropriate areas will strengthen the process of urban bodies integrating their work with that of the Mandal Panchayats.

Smaller Municipalities should be treated at par with Mandal Panchayats for providing benefits flowing through various Special Agencies such as SFDA, MFAL etc. to the people living in these towns.

Panchayati Raj Institutions can assist the Centre and State sector corporations and boards established particularly for commercial activities with promotional and marketing components. In this context, the role of Panchayati Raj Institutions would consist of creating the local organization and locating the area-wise specialties.

Zilla Parishad will be responsible for assessing the over all credit requirements and arranging for its inflow by localizing the needs and locating the areas. The lower tiers should be following this up.

Mandal Panchayats should assist in the establishment of Regional Rural Banks by providing necessary infrastructure and also help the banks in verification procedures or in the analysis of the viability of loan proposals.

III. G.V.K. Rao Committee: 1985

PANCHAYATI RAJ—PAST, PRESENT AND FUTURE

Recognising the importance of democratic institution at grass-root level, Article 40 in Part IV (Directive Principles of State Policy) of the Constitution has stated that the State shall take steps to organize village Panchayats and endow them such powers and authority as may be necessary to enable them to function as units of self-Government. States have established Gram Panchayats of villages or groups of villages with civic and economic activities for a village community as one of the functions.

The Community Development programme was started in 1952 and the Block came to be established as a unit of development administration. It was followed by the National Extension Service to build up an administrative system to tackle the problems of growth and development at the local level. The public participation at the block level was mainly through nominated representatives of the public. It was observed that the public involvement was not effective and the development of a democratic structure of administration from district downwards was felt necessary for meaningful popular participation.

The Balvantrai Mehta Study Team was appointed in 1957 to study the C.D. and NES Programmes, especially from the point of view of assessing the extent of popular participation and to recommend creation of institution through which such participation can be achieved. The Study Team recommended constitution of statutory elective local bodies with the necessary resources, power and authority devolved on them and decentralized administrative system working under their control. It also recommended that the basic unit of democratic decentralization should be located at the block/samiti level. The Study Team envisaged directly elected panchayats for a village or group of villages, an executive body called panchayat samiti for a block with directly elected and co-opted members and an advisory body called Zilla parishad at the district level constituted indirectly, mainly through ex-officio members from lower tier and other with the Collector as Chairman. The National Development Council affirmed the objectives of democratic decentralization and suggested that each Panchayati Raj System and ushering this in Rajasthan, late Pt. Nehru hailed it as "the most revolutionary and historical step in the context of new India".

Panchayati Raj Institutions, being units of local self-Government, come as a State subject under the Constitution and the States and Union Territories are free to design their structure, powers and functions keeping in view their local situations. All States and Union Territories have enacted laws for the establishment of Panchayati Raj Institutions except the State of Meghalaya and Nagaland and Union Territories of Lakshadweep and Mizoram. A three-tier system has been adopted in 12 States and one Union Territory. Two tier system exists in 4 States and 2 Union Territories. There is only one tier of Gram Panchayat in 4 States and 4 Union Territories.

Naturally, members of a Gram Panchayat are elected directly. At the 2nd tier i.e. Block/Tehsil, (except in the case of Assam where it is at sub-division level) there is a mixture of different systems at this level. Five States have provision for direct election; one of them with an indirect election component also. In 5 other States there is indirect election with other representation. In the case of 6 states a body at this level constituted by ex-officio membership from lower tier and others. At the third tier, namely the District level only 5 States have a provision for direct election of its members along with representation of ex-officio and other members. In all other States, the district level body is constituted with ex-officio membership from the lower tier and other representation, with an indirect election component in two States. Thus it can be seen that there is a wide variety in the structure of Panchayati Raj Institutions adopted by different states. The term of office of these bodies is generally 5 years, though there are those with 3, 4, and 6 year terms.

There are over 2,17,300 Village Panchayats in the country covering over 96 per cent of about 5.79 lakhs inhabited villages and 92 per cent of the rural population of the country. On an average a Panchayat covers 2-3 villages and a population of about 2400. There are 4526 Panchayat Samitis (by whatever name called) at the Block/Tehsil level covering 88 per cent of the blocks in the country. On an average a Panchayat Samiti covers about 48 Gram Panchayats. There are 330 Zilla Parishads (by whatever name called) covering about 76 per cent of the districts in the country and each zilla parishad has on an average 13-14 Panchayat Samitis and about 660 Gram Panchayats. There are of course wide local variations.

The functions entrusted to panchayats generally include provision and maintenance of civic services, public hygiene, maintenance of public works like tanks, local irrigation works, community wells, village roads and drainage etc. In some States they are also responsible for primary education, providing inputs for agricultural production, rural industries, primary health care and medical relief, women and child welfare, maintenance of common grazing grounds and other lands and property vested in them. The Panchayat Samitis generally implement various local schemes entrusted to them and some works taken up from their own resources. The Zilla Parishads are generally advisory funds distributing bodies, except in a few States where fairly substantial funds have been placed at their disposal for taking up locally needed schemes.

Bulk of the income of the Panchayati Raj bodies comes from assignments in the land revenue and water rate and/or additional surcharge or cess thereon and various grants by the State Governments. Some revenue is also derived from tax on buildings and non-agricultural lands, the surcharge on stamp duty on transfer of immovable property or on other permitted State taxes, from their vested property, and in some cases from Octroi and assignment of forest revenue etc. The other local taxes, fees, cesses, tolls, license fees etc. on selected professions/trades/callings/industries, water supply, sanitation, lighting, markets, bazars and hats, pilgrims, fairs and festivals, exhibitions, theatrical and cinema shows, rest houses, bus and car stands, vehicles, animals, cattle ponds, slaughter houses, ferries, bridges, cattle grazing, commercial crops etc. permitted in the various State Legislations do not yield much revenue and the bulk of such revenue is at the Gram Panchayat level. In some States Panchayat Samitis and Zila Parishads have no powers of taxation. According to an estimate based on available figures for 1982-83, the total tax revenue realized by Panchayati Raj Institutions constituted a mere 0.1 per cent of all states tax revenue. The tax and non tax income (including grants) realized by the Panchayati Raj institution constituted 4 per cent of the tax and non tax revenue of all States and 3 per cent of all State tax and non tax revenue and capital receipts. Obviously, the resources of the Panchayati Raj institutions are too meager to enable them to discharge effectively the functions which are devolved on or expected of them.

After the initial enthusiasm, following the creation of these institutions, there has been stagnation and later a decline in the functioning of these institutions in many parts of the country, while there are some notable exceptions. Apart from inadequate resources, elections to these bodies have not been held regularly. In fact, elections have becomes overdue for one or more tiers of the Panchayati Raj Institutions in 11 States and in 8 States elections to Gram Panchayats are overdue. Elections have been put off on one pretext on another like drought, floods, census, general elections, delimitation reservation etc. and the term of the existing bodies have been extended or the bodies have been superseded. The Sixth Plan objective of strengthening the process of democratic decentralization, devolving on them such functions which are capable of being planned and implemented at the respective levels, and involving them in the planning and execution of Integrated Rural Development Programme, National Rural Employment Programme, District and Block-level planning and the Minimum

Needs Programmes has had partial success. Wherever the Panchayati Raj bodies have been actively involved, the implementation of rural development programmes has been decidedly better and the selection of beneficiaries and designing of schemes have been more satisfactory.

It is generally accepted that the programmes of rural development will become realistic and meaningful only if people's representatives are actively involved in the local level planning, design, formulation and implementation of these schemes and in selection of beneficiaries in the anti-poverty and employment programmes. In order that the felt needs of the local people and the area are articulated for planning, priorities are established and effectively implemented, there is no better instrument to meet this need other than Panchayati Raj Institutions. These institutions need to be revitalized and endowed with necessary resources and powers to discharge the functions and responsibilities assigned to them.

The committee noted that the Prime Minister has also written to all the Chief Ministers in this regard and requested them to hold regular elections to the Panchayati Raj bodies whenever due, give them administrative power and financial back-up to make them vibrant instruments of popular participation in the development process. It is only through regular elections and ensuring of continued existence and functioning of democratically elected local level bodies that responsible public opinion can be generated and the local bodies become responsive to the needs of the people of the area effective and meaningful in the planning and implementation process. Recently Shri R. Venkataraman while delivering the G.B. Pant Memorial Lecture said: "Panchayati Raj Institutions, for instance, were consciously thought of and devised as a means of remaining informal and of obtaining people's participation. In many States election have not been held to the Panchayat at the Gram or the Zila level for ten years or more. This had the effect of isolating our plans from the beneficiaries of the plans. People have not been involved in the formulation, monitoring and implementation of our plans. The distortions in the planning process are as a result of the neglect of our Panchayati Raj Institutions has serious consequences, "I feel that Constitution should be amended and elections to Panchayats should be compulsory as in the case of State legislatures and Parliament. That is the only way to ensure people's participation in the Planning process." It was in the year 1956 that late Pt. Nehru launched the Panchayati Raj movement. Three decades have elapsed since then and the time has come to have a fresh look at these institutions and re-activate them.

The Ashoka Mehta Committee which reviewed the situation in 1978 to recommend an institutional design for Panchayati Raj in the light of the development thrust and technical expertise required for planning and implementation of rural development programmes commented: "The inescapable compulsion is that the district be the first point for decentralization, under popular supervision, below the State level." District has come to be recognized as a viable administrative unit at which planning, co-ordination and resource allocation are feasible and technical expertise is available. A higher level of popular leadership can also emerge at this level.

The World Conference on Agrarian Reforms and Rural Development held in 1979 under the auspices of the FAO has recommended a programme of action which includes decentralization of institutions and process of government decision making and delegation to institutions of local government, increasing responsibility for decision making in rural development activities, in particular the planning, formulation and implementation of development activities and programmes relating to their regions or areas.

Two expert groups have examined the issue of planning at the district-level and below, namely the working Group on Block-level planning by Prof. M.L. Dantwala and the Working Group on District Planning headed by Dr. C. H. Hanumantha Rao, Member, Planning Commission. Both these committees have studied various aspects of decentralized planning at the district and the block levels and have made recommendations which are, by and large, similar. Both groups have recommended that the basic decentralized planning function has to be done at the district level. Expert group on district planning has commended that the institutional framework for district planning should be a social instrument of decision making which should be a happy blend of local autonomy, administrative capability and planning expertise. This committee is in broad agreement with the main recommendations of the two expert groups.

The development strategy of the Seventh Plan aims at a direct attack on the problems of poverty, unemployment and regional imbalances. The success of this depends on effective steps for the decentralization of planning and development administration on the one hand and involvement and participation of the people in the formulation and implementation process through elected grass root level institutions, voluntary agencies as well as organizations of the poor. These will help in enhancing the effectiveness of the poverty alleviation programmes, in minimizing leakages and in integration of these programmes with area development consistent with local needs. Decentralization and democratization are compulsions of rural development. There is no alternative to raising the awareness of the rural poor and activating and involving representative institutions from below (village panchayats, panchayat samitis, zilla parishads) in the planning and implementation of rural development programmes in an integrated manner for optimal use of resources and for closer monitoring. This is particularly emphasized in the context of special programmes of poverty alleviation and the provision of minimum needs.

The community development programme was essentially in the area of development programme intended to provide institutionalized socio-economic facilities. The creation of the block machinery was a significant step forward in development administration to give an integrated structure to take a total view of the development of an area. But over the years, this has got eroded by the introduction of a multiplicity of sectoral and special programmes, with a proliferation of departmental functionaries both at the district level and at the block level. There has been little coordination in their work and the activities have become fragmented and compartmentalized. Even the setting up of District Rural Development Agencies and the strengthening of the blocks under IRDP have not resulted in the needed integration or overall coordination at the district-block level and there are a number of instances in which a battery of schemes/projects/programmes aimed at the same target group or the same geographical areas, being planned and implemented by independent agencies in a totally un-coordinated manner. The poverty alleviation programmes and the minimum needs programmes are two main sets of programmes which need to be planned and implemented in a closely coordinated and integrated manner along with infrastructure and other development programmes. Such a filed level coordination and integration is conspicuous by its absence. The Community Development and Panchayati Raj Institutions have performed only a limited and peripheral role in local level integrated planning.

Growth with social justice and poverty alleviation continues to be emphasized in the Seventh Five Year Plan. Studies have shown that poverty has tended to diminish where growth has been sustained over along period and, by and large, there has been a positive association between reduction in rural poverty and improved agricultural performance. It is also seen that the percentage of persons below the poverty line in rural areas has tended to increase when the per capita agricultural production has decreased. However, the 'trickle down' of the benefits of growth for alleviation of poverty has not been significant and therefore, a strategy of direct attack on poverty through a pull up measure has been implemented with significant results.

Development experience in the past has clearly indicated that gains from growth, by and large, flow in proportion to the existing asset holdings. Experience of some countries has shown that a more equitable distribution of assets at the start of the growth process will generally result in the new incomes being distributed better. The major asset in the rural areas being land, effective implementation of land reforms has got a crucial importance in this context. There is still a highly skewed distribution of land holdings. According to the agricultural census of 1980-81 of operational holdings of 2 ha. and below (small and marginal) were 66.6 million (74.5 per cent of the total number) operating an area of 42.76 million ha. (26.3 per cent of the total area) whereas operational holdings of 10 ha. and above (large) were 2.15 million (2.4 per cent of the total number) operating an area of 37.13 million ha. (22.8 per cent of the total area). Apart from the fact, due to various reasons, the declared surplus land is far less than the estimated surplus land is involved in litigation.

Ownership rights have not been completed on tenants in some States. In many parts of the country there are insecure tenants and share-croppers. The success of the strategy of increasing agricultural production and asset endowment to the rural poor for income generating activities depend on effective land and tenurial reforms. Even marginal and sub-marginal land would be of much importance to the poor. Even for non-land based activities possession of a certain minimum land holding would be desirable. The seventh five year plan has stated that land reforms should be an intrinsic part of the anti-poverty strategy. Redistributive land reforms and bringing on record oral, informal and insecure tenants to provide security of tenure followed by conferment of ownership have to be pushed through. The involvement of Panchayati Raj Institutions in this process would be of considerable importance, as experience has shown. Assistance to assigns of surplus land should be integrated with the programme of IRDP, NREP etc. The developmental role of the Revenue Department in this regard is also to be recognized, especially in the context of maintenance of up-to-date land and crop records required for various purposes like land reforms, flow of agricultural credit, food procurement, social forestry etc. apart from the requirements of planning.

The importance of anti-poverty programme in rural development has to be considered in the correct perspective. Measures of poverty alleviation, whether it be through an asset endowment under IRDP or provision of wage income through NREP/RLEGP or drought proofing under the area development programmes of DPAP and DDP have to be integrated with the Minimum Needs Programme, as they are mutually supportive. The Seventh Five Year Plan has emphasized this aspect and urged the creation of the necessary linkages between beneficiary and area development oriented anti-poverty programmes of rural development and the Minimum Needs Programme components of human resources and area development.

Indeed it is necessary that such integration and establishment of linkages are given a concrete shape. Infrastructural development on an integrated area basis is essential. For example, agriculture and dairy development schemes have to be linked with provision of inputs and credit, communication, roads, markets, rural electrification etc. Livestock development has to be connected with animal health cover and pasture and fodder development. Irrigation should cover catchments area treatment to command area development. Watershed development should encompass soil and water conservation, ground water exploitation, dry land farming technology, pasture and fodder development and afforestation. It is well-known that education of girls and women, nutrition, rural health and sanitation and rural water supply have a very significant role to play in the family welfare programmes and to achieve the small family norm. Forest development through farm forestry and social forestry has to give emphasis on fuel wood and fodder to meet the requirement of rural domestic cooking energy and a large livestock population. The complementarity of the activities and the supplemental role of the funds from different sources can be properly realized only if an integrated area planning can be done at the district level. With the shift in emphasis from multi-area sectoral programmes to multi-sectoral area programmes and projectisation, the technical expertise required for such an exercise can only be found at the district level and not below. Effective horizontal coordination between different agencies would be possible under a single umbrella body at the district level with a dynamic leadership.

There are large number of small schemes which are vital to the poor and of great utility to agricultural development but inadequate attention is bestowed on them. Examples are, small minor irrigation schemes, soil and water conservation including check dams and water harvesting structures, community irrigation wells etc. Equally important are certain functions where the border line between maintenance and development is rather thin, for example, provision of equipment to schools, drugs to dispensaries etc. Then there are maintenance functions that are often neglected—maintenance of roads, buildings, water supply schemes and hand pumps etc. Devolving these to the district level will help in giving greater attention, better planning and more effective and purposeful management. While the distinction between plan and non-plan can get blurred at the district level with a district budget, care should, however, be exercised to see that funds meant for maintenance do not get diverted, as improper and inadequate maintenance will prove much more expensive in the long run.

An organizational structure requires to be built up for integrated planning, effective implementation, better management, closer monitoring and concurrent evaluation to ensure optimal use of resources and delivery of benefits to those for whom they are meant. This should also keep in view national objectives, state priorities, regional requirements; local needs and people's aspirations. The structure at the district-level will, therefore, have a dual function of integrated area planning and effective implementation.

States have been generally lukewarm to the purpose of democratic decentralization. In most States the Panchayati Raj bodies have been allowed to languish without powers and resources. Development has come of age and the time has come to take the planning, decision-making and implementation process nearer to the people through democratic bodies. The inevitable need to transfer power of the State to democratic bodies at the local level has to be recognized. Inadequacies in the present system have to be remedied and a participative feeling in the gigantic task of rural development and poverty alleviation needs to be generated. The rural development administration has to become poor-oriented in its attitudes, procedures and processes. A unified development administration structure has to be brought in at the district level and below. A quantum jumps in organizational design required to meet these tasks is now not only opportune but also ineluctable.

The Committee is of the opinion that there should be a significant decentralisation at the district level. There should be a district level body, say, the Zila Parishad for the rural areas, with directly elected members at the rate of one member for every 30,000 to 40,000 population, with suitable scaling down for sparsely populated and hilly areas. Representative of the District Co-operative Bank, urban local self-Government institutions as well as members of the Legislative Assembly and Parliament may also be associated with this body. Adequate representation should also be provided for under-privileged economic/occupational/social groups including Scheduled Castes, Scheduled Tribes and women as well as for organization of the poor, if there be such bodies. The Committee noted that the recent Karnataka Legislation has provided 25 per cent reservation for women. The term of Zila parishad should be from 3 to 5 years. Election should be held regularly whenever it becomes due. They should not be normally superseded and even if it is done under extraordinary circumstances, it should not be more than 6 months, within which time fresh elections should be conducted.

So far as the office of the Chairman of Zila Parishad is concerned, States could adopt one of two models. He could be elected from among its own members for the term of the Zila Parishad. However, in order to give a greater sense of participative feeling and to avoid growth of frictional power centres, the alternative model of the mayoral pattern with an elected Chairman holding office for one year is commended by the Committee for consideration of the States. The election in both cases of the Chairman and the Vice-Chairman, if there be one, could by the mechanism of a single transferable vote. The Chairman and the members of the Zila Parishad would also need to be given orientation/training which should be organized by the National Institute of Rural Development, Hyderabad.

All the Developmental Departments with their line information at the district level and below should be brought squarely under the Zila Parishad. The budgets, non-plan and plan, of these departments and the funds for various special schemes implemented at the district level or below should be transferred to Zila Parishad to form the district budget. In implementation, of course, the norms and guidelines for the various special programmes should be adhered to and the funds for these should not be divertible. The planning exercise will have to mesh them and the various sectoral and area development programmes into a mosaic and draw up a comprehensive design of integrated development of each area. An illustrative list of departments which can be placed under the Zila Parishad is given below:

1. Agriculture including soil conservation, horticulture.
2. Animal husbandry and veterinary services, fisheries.
3. Co-operation.
4. Minor irrigation and ground water development
5. Primary and adult education.

6. Public health and family welfare including primary health centres.
7. Rural water supply and sanitation.
8. District and rural roads and departments buildings in district (PWD).
9. Small scale and rural industries (District industries centre).
10. Welfare of Scheduled Castes and Scheduled Tribes.
11. Social and women welfare including children.
12. Social Forestry (from Forestry Department).

The officers of the line departments will continue to discharge functions devolved on them by statutes. However, the States will have to work out suitable arrangements for delineation of work between the Zila Parishad and other statutory authorities, such as the Command Area Development Authority which may be operating in the same area.

The Zila Parishads may operate through various committees. They should be compact and in order to ensure participation of all the members of the Zila Parishad in one Committee or other, the members of the committee should be elected by the members of the Zila Parishad from among themselves in accordance with the system of proportional representation by means of single transferable vote. The Committee suggests the following typical committees of the Zila Parishad:

1. General Standing Committee to look after establishment and miscellaneous residuary matters.
2. Finance and Audit Committee to look after finances, framing of budgets, considering proposals for increase in revenue, consideration of proposals affecting finances, examination of receipts and expenditure, internal audit.
3. Planning Committee to look after integrated planning including co-operative and other credit planning as well as area development programmes of DPAP/DDP where existing, statistics evaluation of programmes and schemes.
4. Anti-Poverty Programme Committee to look after the programmes of IRDP, NREP, RLEGP etc., as also employment generating works under drought relief.
5. Public Works and Amenities Committee to look after minor

irrigation, district and rural roads, buildings, rural housing, village extensions, rural water supply, ground water development, rural electrification etc.

6. Agricultural and Animal Husbandry Committee to look after agriculture (including seed farms, provision of seeds and fertilizers, crop protection), soil and water conservation, agricultural extension, dry land development command area development, horticulture, livestock development, animal health, and veterinary services, pasture and fodder development, fisheries, cooperative societies etc.
7. Education Committee to look after primary and adult education except academic matter.
8. Health Committee to look after hospitals and dispensaries including primary health centres below district level, nutrition, rural health and sanitation, rural water supply and family welfare schemes.
9. Industries Committee to look after small-scale, village and cottage industries, promotion, training, provision of inputs and marketing.
10. Social Forestry Committee to look after the programmes of farm forestry, social forestry and the new Minimum Needs Programme of Rural Domestic Cooking Energy.
11. Social Justice Committee to look after institutions and programmes for welfare of Schedule Castes, Scheduled Tribes, social and women's welfare and schemes for other weaker sections of the society.

It would be seen from the above that all the basic developmental departments and programmes including the anti-poverty programmes and the Minimum Needs Programme which are vital to rural development come squarely under the Zila Parishad with non-official leadership for integrated and harmonized functioning. The Planning and decision making process will be effectively decentralized. The various developmental departments will provide the technical expertise required for planning and function under the supervision of the concerned committees. With democratic decentralization of development functions on the lines suggested above, one can say that country will be taking the first important step towards a district government.

In order that the objective of planning from below is achieved and felt needs of the people and the area are catered to, it would also be desirable to provide a certain sectorally unallocated lumpsum to each Zila Parishad. The determination of such amounts to be provided by the State Government could be entrusted to a Finance Commission to be appointed by each Government say, once in 5 years.

It is also to be recognized that the needs of the district as they would emerge in the District Plans prepared by the Zila Parishads could be far more than what the resources would permit. It is also possible that the perception of priorities at district level could be such that, added together, the amounts required for these would be much larger than the amounts that can be allocated under the State Plan with its priorities. A mechanism for harmonizing these would also be necessary. The Committee suggests that there should be a State Development Council for the purpose with the Chief Minister as the Chairman. All the Ministers of Government and Chairman of Zila Parishads could be its members. The Development Commissioner could be its Secretary. The State Development Council could meet as often as necessary. Among its functions could be the approval of district plans as well as approval of the State Annual Plan prepared by meshing together the district plans and other sectoral plans.

At the level lower than that of the district, two different models are available for consideration of the state Governments. The Block has come to be recognized as a development administration unit and integrated area planning can also start at the block level for preparation of District Plans ultimately. The Committee has also envisaged restoration of original concept of integrated development at the Block level which was conceived for the Community Development Programme and providing administrative leadership at this level higher than prevalent at present. The Committee also recommends that there should be a directly elected body, say the Panchayat Samiti, to be responsible for planning and implementation of developmental schemes under the guidance of the Zila Parishad. There should be reservation on this body for the Scheduled Castes, Scheduled Tribes, women etc. The body at this level should also have representatives of Marketing Cooperative

Societies and Land Development Banks operating at the Block level. The line Department operating at the Block level should function under the Panchayat Samiti. The Panchayat Samiti should get Block plans prepared for its approval. The Panchayat Samiti will also have executive functions in implementation of the schemes as also final selection of beneficiaries under IRDP etc. Below the level the existing structure of directly elected Gram Panchayats will continue.

Another model which may be considered is the constitution of mandal Panchayats for a group of villages with a population 15,000 to 20,000 instead of the present Gram Panchayats. This should have directly elected members with reservations for Scheduled Castes, Scheduled Tribes, women etc. This could be an executive body entrusted with schemes which can be implemented at the level. They could also be involved in the selection of beneficiaries for anti-poverty and employment programmes. In this model the States may also like to have a Panchayat Samiti at the Block level as an Advisory-Cum Co-ordinating body constituted indirectly from representatives of Mandal Panchayats, Zila Parishads, members of area cooperative institutions etc. which could also be responsible for getting Block plans prepared.

There should be a Gram Sabha for each village consisting of all voters of village. This should meet as often as necessary but the interval between any two consecutive meetings should not be more than 6 months. The meeting should be presided over by the Chairman or in his absence, the Vice-Chairman of the Gram Panchayat or the Mandal Panchayat, as the case may be. The identification of beneficiaries under poverty alleviation programmes like IRDP, NERP, RLEGP etc. should be done in Gram Sabha meetings. The Panchayat should place before the Gram Sabha a report about development programmes taken up for the village during the previous year and proposals for the current year for their consideration. The Gram Sabha can give proposals for new programmes and also help in organizing various activities in the village. The recommendations of the Gram Sabha should be given due consideration by the Gram/Mandal Panchayat, Panchayat Samiti and Zila Parishad.

The Panchayat Samiti and the Gram/Mandal Panchayat should have a sub-committee, consisting mainly of women members, for considering and implementing programmes and schemes for welfare of woman and children, including adult education.

Many villages and towns have untapped human resources like retired persons with technical or other expertise willing to offer their services and also persons who are active in social work. There should be provision to co-opt or associate such persons or representatives of voluntary agencies or of organizations of the poor on the relevant committees of the Panchayati Raj Institutions. Voluntary agencies operating in different areas and organizations of the poor should also be involved in the developmental programmes in a large measure.

IV. L.M. Singhvi Committee: 1986

REVITALISATION OF PRIS FOR DEMOCRACY AND DEVELOPMENT

The concept of Panchayats was a part of the philosophy of 'Purna Swaraj' and 'Gram Swaraj'. Mahatma Gandhi and Jawaharlal Nehru breathed into those concepts an inexorable and practical patriotic impetus during the era of India's struggle for independence. Indeed, at the seed time of our Constitution, the concept of village panchayats was not a remote and hoary historical concept. It was a part of the legacy of India's struggle for freedom and its quest for its own traditions and identity.

The Constitution of India was enacted, adopted and proclaimed in the name of the people of India as an organic document of democratic self-government and rule of law enshrines for democratic faith and resolve of the resurgent people of India committed to the philosophy of "Swaraj" not only in the sense of emancipation from the colonial yoke of an alien imperial power but in the sense of self-government and the protection of the fundamental rights and dignity of the individual as a way of life and social habit. The fabric of our constitutional philosophy is woven with the warp and woof of democracy and rule of law.

The Constitution of India provides for republican democracy at the national level in the form of its bicameral Parliament and by making the Council of Ministers collectively responsible to the House of the People. The same basic pattern of parliamentary institutions is replicated at the level of States which form the Union of India. In the quasifederal framework of India's Parliamentary democracy, the creation of Panchayati Raj Institutions and their organization was, however, left to a general directive embodied in Article 40 of the Constitution in the following terms:

> Organization of Village Panchayats—The State shall take steps to organize Village Panchayats and endow them with such powers and authority as may be necessary to enable them to function as units of self-government.

Article 40 came to be discussed and inserted somewhat belatedly on 22nd November, 1948 as Article 31 (A) in the Draft Constitution of India and now renumbered as Article 40 in the Chapter IV of the Constitution of India. It is significant to recall that at one point of time, the omission of village panchayats from the draft constitution was sought to be justified on the ground that the village communities in India which had survived through many vicissitudes were not fit to be units of self-government. On that issue, there was considerable furore and ferment among Members of the Constituent Assembly. A modus vivendi was then worked out behind the scenes. As a result, Shri K. Santhanam's amendment which eventually became article 40 of the Constitution came to be accepted in a somewhat reticent and quiescent manner. No controversial statements were made. The debate in the Constituent Assembly on this provision occupies less than eight pages and does not fully reflect the range of conflict out of which the accord was fashioned. Earlier, Dr. Rajendra Prasad has also expressed the view somewhat wistfully that the Constituent Assembly should have attempted to adopt village republics as the basis of the Constitution. The Constitutional Advisor, Shri Benegal Narasing Raju, while sympathizing with the idea, has pointed out that it was too late to make an attempt to change the basis of the Constitution, the preparation of which had already progressed considerably. As Shri T. Prakasam implied during the debate in the Constituent Assembly Shri K. Santhanam's amendment was belated but welcome attempt to salvage the Constitution from the fundamental standpoint of Mahatma Gandhi's philosophy of grass-root democracy. In the speeches made in the Constituent Assembly, there were echoes of the Gandhian concept of village self-government and eloquent references to India's ancient republican and democratic traditions.

Clearly, the inclusion of Article 40 as a Directive Principle of State policy did not more than accommodate a conceptual viewpoint. It did not enact it in a mandatory and constitutive form as an integral and operating part of the constitution. Article 40, however, does contain in it the seeds of a constitutional mandate and unequivocally projects the concept of village panchayats as units of self-government and requires that they should be endowed with all necessary powers and authority to enable them to function as units of self-government.

The true potential of Article 40 lies not merely in its directive to the Indian State at all levels as a part of constitutionally formulated principle of State Policy to organize village panchayats but in its significant concomitant mandate that panchayat should be endowed with "such powers and authority as may be necessary to enable them to function as units of self-government". The message of that mandate is clear and clarion. It means that the task and the tryst of the founding fathers of the Constitution would remain incomplete unless village panchayats begin to function as units of self-government as a part of our democratic policy. An attempt to conceptualize the framework of panchayat institutions is to take its inspiration from the constitutional mandate to complete that unfinished task. The theological emphasis of that constitutional mandate is structural, operational and functional with its implicit ramifications for our democracy and development, for freedom and welfare, and for justice, liberty, equality, individual dignity, national unity and Indian people's fraternity as integrally correlated concepts.

INTEGRATED VISION OF DEMOCRACY

The National Parliament and the Central Government, the State Legislatures and the State Governments and the whole pyramid of our judicial system are important to the working of democracy and the maintenance of the rule of law. In their own respective spheres, these legislative executive and judicial institutions provide an important infrastructure. To the common Indian villages, however, they do not represent a pre-occupying part of his daily life. The revolution in communication technology does often enough lift and transport him audio-visually to the ambiance of these institutions but he cannot quite relate to them in terms of his daily needs and everyday concerns. Self-government may mean to him only the spectacular occasion when he exercises his franchise; but his participation in the electoral process for the Lok Sabha and the Vidhan Sabha can not give him a sense of full and meaningful participation in the democratic process. He is unable to feel great power and even the greater responsibility of being a citizen in the democratic republic that is India. There are gaps and anomalies in the democratic experience of the Indian citizen, particularly in the countryside. Panchayati Raj Institutions in our rural areas and municipal bodies in our urban areas represent, first and foremost, the possibility of a truly dependable and durable institutional assurance for overcoming those distances and gaps. Without local units of self-government, we can not hope to establish a viable and vibrant democracy. It is in this perspective that rural and urban development are, in effect, two sides of the same coin and are parts of a composite continuum of what may be called democratic urbanization. Self-government necessarily subsumes and supplements developments in all its ramifications in rural as well as urban contexts. It is with an integrated vision that they have to be reviewed, restructured, reclaimed, renewed and revitalized.

The experience of local self-government in the urban areas and in the districts in different parts of India during the period of British rule was uneven. It is true that certain ground rules of municipal self-government were evolved in the cities and towns during that period. Some of the municipal bodies acquitted themselves so creditably that they become examples of civic self-government at its best. There were, however other municipalities which appeared to be insufficiently imbued with the philosophy of local self-government. The District Councils were primarily administrative structures and did not quite come into their own. One of the obvious reasons was that the country was dominated by colonial administration and its pre-emptive imperatives. In the countryside, panchayats were quite often caste institutions with a pivotal social role but they did not function as institutions of State and instruments of self-government and social change.

The constitutional vision of republican self-government at the village level enshrined in Article 40 came to be unfolded a few years after the commencement of our constitution when it became increasingly self-evident that community development and socio-economic transformation could not be achieved without democratic participation. This compelling and inescapable realization of the limitations of the bureaucratic models led to an enthusiastic interest in Panchayati Raj Institutions which was enlivened by generous impulses.

The Community Development Programme was launched in 1952. The blocks came to be established as units of development administration. The National Extension Service was established soon thereafter with a view to reinforce the administrative network to tackle the problems of growth and development at different local and functional levels. At that stage there was, relatively speaking, only nominal public participation through nominated representatives of the public. Soon, lack of public involvement and participation began to be perceived as an impediment in the successful implementation of the Community Development and National Extension Service Programmes. Based on that perception, the Second Plan document recognized the necessity for speeding up the development of democratic institutions and concluded that "unless there is a comprehensive village planning, which takes into account the needs of the entire community, weaker sections like tenant-cultivators, landless workers and artisans may not benefit sufficiently from assistance provided by the Government". Referring to the aim of the National Extension Movement to reach every family in the village, the Second Five Year Plan reported that in order to fulfill that aim it was necessary to have "an agency in the village which represents the community as a whole and can assume responsibility and initiative for developing the resources of the village and providing the necessary leadership. Indeed, rural progress depends entirely on the existence of an active organization in the village which can bring all the people including the weaker sections mentioned above into common programmes to be carried out with the assistance of the administration". The idea behind the Second Plan was that village panchayats along with co-operatives could play a considerable part in bringing about a more just and integrated social structure in rural areas. The thrust of the Second Five Year Plan was to establish statutory panchayats in all the villages though more as vehicles for national extension and community development projects and not so much as units of self-government. It was primarily from this angle that the number of panchayats was to be more than doubled by 1960-61.

This Committee is of view that it has been a fundamental error to regard Panchayati Raj Institutions primarily as convenient tools for administrative programmes and development projects. That error had the effect, in greater or lesser measure, of devaluing and downgrading the role of these institutions as units of self-government and relegating them to a secondary position, harming and hampering both democracy and development.

ASCENT AND ENNUI OF PANCHAYATI RAJ MOMENTUM

The Balwantrai Mehta Team was appointed in January, 1957 to study and report on the Community Development Projects and National Extension Service with a view to "economy and efficiency" and, among others "for the assessment of the extent to which the movement has succeeded in utilizing local initiative and in creating institutions to ensure continuity in the process of improving economic and social conditions in rural areas". Once again the approach was primarily to achieve economy and efficiency. The Balwantrai Mehta Team, however, found that "Development can not progress without responsibility and power. Community Development can be real only when the community understands its problems; realizes its responsibilities, exercises the necessary powers through its chosen representatives and maintains a constant and intelligent vigilance on local administration". It was with this objective that the team recommended an early establishment or statutory elective local bodies and devolution to them of the necessary resources, powers and authority.

The recommendations of the Balwantrai Mehta Study Team came as a fresh breeze and gave a new lease to community development and extension service projects. It paved the way for a new era of Panchayati Raj Institutions which was inaugurated by Pandit Jawaharlal Nehru on 2nd October, 1959 at a National rally at Nagur.

Pandit Jawaharlal Nehru described the new beginning as "the most revolutionary and historical step in the context of new India". In a sense, it was an act of faith in republican democracy and was as important an event as the establishment of the parliamentary system itself for the people of India and by the people of India. The idea rode on the crest of the new wave of public enthusiasm which had found a sense of direction and an institutional habitat. The spirited launching of Panchayati Raj Institutions at Nagur seemed to capture the public imagination. That memorable rally aroused high hopes and great expectations. The idea was not meant to be a mere counsel of convenience or as a design of an auxiliary system of development administration. Indeed, the momentum of that momentous change was lost and the Panchayati Raj Institutions began to decline when their status and role as units of self-government were eclipsed by a combination of several factors of decadence and disarray. When the basic premise of Panchayati Raj Institutions as units of self-government was lost, these institutions also lost their capability to fulfil as the promise of development.

After the Balwantrai Mehta Study Team reported, legislation was enacted in different States except in the State of Meghalaya and Nagland and UTs of Lakshadweep and Mizoram. According to the Committee set up by the Planning Commission which reported in December 1985, a three-tier system has been adopted in 12 states and one Union Territory, two-tier system exists in 4 states and 2 union territories. Electoral system also differs from states to state. In terms of structures, electoral procedures, powers and functions, there is a considerable variety in the Panchayat institutions adopted by the States. There are, today, more than 2,17,300 village panchayats in the country covering over 96% of about 5.79 lakhs inhabited villages and 92% of the rural population of our country. There are about 4526 panchayat samitis of different nomenclature at the block, taluka or tehsil level. There are about 330 Zila Parishad covering about 76% of the district in the country; each Zila Parishad has on an average 13 to 14 Panchayati Samitis and about 660 Gram Panchayats.

Though there are variations from state to state, it may be broadly stated that the functions entrusted to panchayats include village roads, community wells, maintenance of public parks, tanks, irrigation works, public hygiene, drainage and other civil services. In some states, they are also responsible for primary education and are entrusted with functions relating to rural industries, primary health care, medical relief, women and child welfare, maintenance of common grazing grounds and other community lands and properties and provision of inputs of agricultural production. The extent and tempo of the involvement of Panchayati Raj Institutions in basic planning and implementation of development projects is also subject to wide variations from State to State and even within the States. Most Panchayati Raj Institutions appear to suffer from grave insufficiency of resources which generally devolve upon them from assignments in the land revenue and water rate, or additional surcharge on cess on land revenue and water rate and various grants by the State Governments. In some cases revenue is derived from octroi and assignment of forest revenue. Some of the Panchayati Raj Institutions also derive income from taxes on buildings and non-agricultural lands or from surcharge on stamp duty on transfer of immovable property. Variable in terms of yield, but not unimportant in the lives of Indians in rural areas, there are local taxes, fees, cesses, tolls, licence fees and other similar levies, on trades, industries, water supply, sanitation, lighting, markets, bazars and hats, pilgrims, fairs and festivals, exhibitions, entertainment shows, rest houses, bus stands, car stands, camel parking, vehicle parking, animals, cattle ponds, fish ponds, slaughter houses, ferries, bridges, cattle grazing lands and commercial crops. The list of subjects on which levies may be made may not appear to suffer from brevity but the sum total of yields and collections do suffer from chronic paucity particularly in the context of the responsibilities which are or ought to be entrusted to Panchayati Raj Institutions and their significant bearing on the quality of life in our rural areas.

The network of Panchayati Raj Institutions covers the length and breadth of the country today but not in the sense and manner they were meant to. Numerically and quantitatively there are myriads of these institutions dotting the entire landscape of our country.

Powers and functions have been conferred on them by legislative enactments. There is, however, a feeling that these institutions have become moribund and that they have been denuded of their promise and vitality. There is a legitimate question mark against these institutions, not because the constitutional promise has been abandoned nor because self-government is no longer an article of faith with us, not because we have lost faith in ourselves; but because we have allowed these institutions to be neglected, because we have failed to nurture them with the inputs and material and human resources necessary for them and because the operational claims and quest of political power have taken a heavy toll on the fundamental concept of self-government and public services.

Initially democracy and development seemed to march hand in hand. There was climate of optimism and resurgence, but within a few years of the inauguration of the new era, Panchayati Raj institutions began to sag, stagnate and decline.

The potential of Panchayati Raj Institutions as centres of people's power aroused apprehensions and a jealous hostility all around. Elected representatives in Parliament and State Legislatures saw with dismay their inevitable dependence on Panchayati Raj functionaries with whom they were not quite willing to share power. There was public apathy and indifference and a perceptible weakening of political will to support these institutions on a priority basis. There was chronic insufficiency of resources at the disposal of these institutions. Most of these institutions had to function in a hand to mouth predicament in a state of perpetual neglect and humiliated impoverishment. The bureaucracy was becoming alienated after the initial phase and had begun to resort to systematic by-passing of these institutions. Programme after programme was launched without involving Panchayati Raj Institutions in them. These programmes have become close preserves of bureaucracy undermining and frustrating the Panchayati Raj Institutions as units of local self-government. Facilities for training were meager. Research and reform inputs were negligible. Political factionalism and certain public disenchantment with these institutions weakened them further and these institutions failed to nourish themselves from the reserviour of people's power because Gram Sabha as a basic institution did not become a living and pulsating reality. Corruption began to creep in. What is worse, elections to Panchayati Raj Institutions were not held for years together. Elected Sarpanches and Panches and other Panchayati Raj functionaries were suspended and Panchayati Raj Institutions were superseded frequently and indiscriminately.

This is a formidable catalogue of causes. These were and continue to be more than merely symptomatic maladies or minor ailments. These ailments which have afflicted Panchayati Raj Institutions for nearly a quarter of century are primarily the ailments of our body politic. From the very start, it was an onerous struggle for survival for the Panchayati Raj Institutions in the face of hostile and adverse encounter with institutions of established power. Unfortunately, the elected political elite as well as the entrenched bureaucracy saw in the emerging leadership of Panchayati Raj Institutions a competing cadre with whom they were not particularly anxious to socialize or co-operate. The State Governments which were primarily responsible for nurturing these institutions began to look askance at them. Not surprisingly, these institutions also suffered from begnin neglect at the national level, although occasional expressions of concern were not lacking. These expressions, however, proved to be cries in the wilderness.

This committee is of the view that Panchayati Raj Institutions declined because of lack of conceptual clarity, absence of political will and denial of national priority, lack of continuous process of research, evaluation, feed back and correction at these institutions in a blind alley.

The Committee is of the opinion that the quantitative and geographical expanse of Panchayati Raj Institutions throughout the country is not necessarily an asset, unless we set about purposefully to change their orientation. These institutions can be turned to good account but there are Augean stables which cannot be cleansed except by turning the waters of the river Alpheas through them. The concept of grass-root democracy for its own sake and the concept of development as an integral part of self-government can be durable inputs of catalysis and chatharsis to make Panchayat Raj Institutions fully effective and credible.

AN APPROACH TO CONCEPTUALISATION

First and foremost, this committee conceptualizes the Panchayati Raj Institution as basic units of self-government. The Committee takes the Indian villages and the Gram Sabha as the republican base of our democratic nation. The Committee considers the Gram Sabha as the embodiment of direct democracy.

The Committee believes that the concept of Panchayati Raj Institutions must draw its inspiration from the quintessential concept of Gram Swaraj. That is the explicit mandate and background of article 40 of the Constitution. The Committee is of the view that the concept of village panchayats as units of self-government is central and integral to the Constitutional mandate and is vital in terms of the living rural reality. The committee is of the view that villages may be reorganized and many of them may in the process be grouped and enlarged in order to make for more viable village panchayats and enlarged villages should continue to be the primary and homogenous units of self-government with a measure of direct democracy.

The Committee is conscious of the fact that demographic size of villages in our country varies considerably. According to the report of Asoka Mehta Committee, a demographic analysis of our village's shows that 26% of them have population below 200, 52.3% has a population of more than 200 but below 1000. 20.5% of our villages have a population ranging from 1000 to 5000; a little less than 1% of our villages have a population of more than 5000 but below 10000 and nearly 2% of our villages have a population of 10000 and above.

The demographic size of the area is no doubt relevant to the effective transfer of technology, organization of services in respect of health, education, agricultural and industrial sectors and other welfare activities. Rationalization of territorial limits and demographic size is a highly desirable goal in the on-going process of democratic self-government, technology transfer and economic development. The Committee recommends village reorganization in our country on the basis of relevant criteria which should take into account factors of identity, continuity, contiguity, homogeneity, communications and techno-economic, demographic and cultural factures. The

Committee feels that there is a case of larger and more viable village units. Ideally, our Village Panchayats should have a population of five thousand or less but demographic size is only one of the relevant dimensions. These would be the village of the future. The task of delimitation of reorganized villages should be performed preferably by a Commission in each State under the mandate of a statute on the basis of clearly enunciated criteria, the application of which would have to be carefully balanced in the light of public representations and population proclivities. The Committee would, however, caution against the concept of large federal mandal units with numerous hinterland villages as basic units of self-government. Even though federated Mandals may appear to be administratively more efficient from a planning point of view, they will be democratically less self-sufficient and less self-reliant.

Striking a balance between techno-economic viability and village identity in an optimum mix of demographic and geographical size should be a policy goal and practical endeavour keeping in mind that each village must be viewed as unit of self-government. We are of the view that optimization of economic growth and social justice is bound to follow in the wake of village panchayats operating as units of self-government and as cradles of civic culture, social ethos, public education, poverty alleviation programmes, voluntary citizen action and constructive work. It will require considerable patience but it will pay handsome dividends.

The Panchayati Raj Institutions should be organized as a part of the process of democratic decentralization for building up the institutional edifice from the grass-roots upwards and not as a gift of devolutionary process. The Committee is of the view that the Panchayati Raj Institutions have to be viewed as institutions of self-government which would naturally facilitate the participation of the people in the process of planning and development flowing from and as a part of the concept of self-government. Development that bureaucratic structures and devolutionary strategies cannot achieve people's participation in a meaningful manner.

The Committee is of the view that the operational dynamics of Panchayati Raj should be directed to achieve community and social mobilization transcending the barriers of caste, religion, sex and disparities of wealth and surmounting social disabilities and disadvantages. The Panchayati Raj Institutions should become vehicles for homogenization, secularization and socialization of national ethos. This has to be a conscious process through specific programmes and by an effective utilization of the media of mass communication.

NEED FOR CONSTITUTIONAL PROTECTION

The Committee envisages and recommends that local self-government should be constitutionally recognized, protected and preserved by the inclusion of a new chapter in the Constitution. Local self-government and more particularly, Panchayati Raj Institutions, should be constitutionally proclaimed as the third tier of Government. The Committee commends the broad framework and content of the constitutional amendments which were drafted several years ago in 1974-75 by a committee under the Chairmanship of Dr. L.M. Singhvi and comprising, Shri S.K. Dey (Formerly Minister of Community Development) and Shri R.C.S. Sarkar (former Law Secretary and Chairman of Union Public Service Commission) as a starting point. The Committee is of the view that a separate chapter should be added in the Constitution so as to make the identity and integrity of the Panchayati Raj Institutions reasonably and substantially inviolate.

The Committee viewed with concern the peculiar phenomenon of elections to Panchayati Raj bodies not being held for years after the expiry of their statutory terms in most states. The magnitude of delay in holding elections was shocking and staggering in many cases. Without the renewal of their mandate, the Panchayati Raj Institutions become empty shells or mere wire pulling mechanisms. An electoral mandate is evidently the life breath of a democratic institution. To deprive the Panchayati Raj Institutions of that life breath was to suffocate and asphyxiate them.

The committee is of the view that elections to Panchayati Raj bodies should be held promptly at the end of the specified term. A Constitutional provision should be made to ensure regular, free and fair elections for Panchayati Raj bodies and the task should be entrusted to the Election Commission of India operating through State Commissions or similar apparatus. No Panchayati Raj Institution should be allowed to remain superseded for more than six or seven months. These elections should be held on the basis of the electoral rolls which are prepared for the Lok Sabha and State Assemblies.

The Committee feels that in order to avoid apprehensions and charges of political bias or interference, it would favorably consider recommendation for a Panchayati Raj Judicial Tribunal to be constituted in each State to adjudicate controversies in relation to elections, suspensions, super sessions, dissolutions and other matters relating to the working of Panchayati Raj Institutions and its elected personnel.

The Committee is of the considered view that ways and means should be found to ensure the availability of adequate financial resources for Panchayati Raj Institutions to function effectively. The Committee notes that institutions of local self-government have often been reluctant to raise revenue resources by the exercise of their taxing powers. The Committee views this tendency with concern and hopes that this would be overcome progressively. The committee would suggest a pattern of compulsory and optional levies and a list of subjects in respect of which powers to levy taxes and fees may be entrusted to Panchayati Raj Institutions with a provision that for a given period, the State Governments shall levy and collect on behalf of Panchayati Raj Institutions and shall disburse to them, on the basis of the recommendation of Finance Commission in each State. The Committee also suggests that the Finance Commission appointed by the Union Government under the Constitution should make an adequate earmarked provision for Panchayati Raj Institutions. The Committee further recommends that resources budgeted for various rural development and poverty alleviation programmes should be routed through Panchayati Raj Institutions which would as a result gain in authority sand effectiveness.

PARTY POLITICS AND PANCHAYATI RAJ

The Committee is of the view that it is neither practicable nor desirable to injunct the participation of individuals associated with political parties in Panchayati Raj Institutions by law. If a consensus is not reached and if elections are held, it does not decisively change the situation merely to provide by law that no party symbols will be allotted in the elections, so long as parties in fact remain active in the electoral process. Indeed there is something to be said in such a situation; to allow the cleansing symbolises of open electoral competition and contest which is otherwise a part of national politics. The Committee feels that the role of political parties or self-denying self-restraint by political parties in that respect has to be evolved by a consensus among the political parties rather than making it a subject matter of legislative prohibition. Perhaps the issue should be thrashed out by the Prime Minister in the National Development Council and in consultation with leaders of different political parties. In this respect the Committee awaits responses, from political parties and others so that a pragmatic, workable and consensual recommendations may be made by the Committee. In this respect, the present situation calls for a candid and forthright re-appraisal.

NYAYA PANCHAYATS

The committee is of the view that the institutions of Nyaya Panchayats are a valuable aid to the development of social habits of self-government and rule of law. Nyaya Panchayats should be entrusted with the functions of mediation and conciliation in addition to adjudication. The Committee suggests that there may be a Nyaya Panchayat for a cluster of villages constituted by election or appointed from a special panel to be prepared for the purpose. In addition, each party to the dispute may be permitted to choose a Nyaya Panch from a panel to be presided by a professional judge as in the case of arbitration proceedings. Alternatively they may be elected by a consensus in primary Panchayat units so far as possible. It is suggested that appropriate qualification and training may also be prescribed and a permanent staff for keeping records and for service of notices of summons should be appointed. In this connection, the Committee would like to consider the full implications and ramifications of the recent recommendations of the Law Commission in respect of another variant of local in the form of Gram Nyayalayas.

A PLEA FOR INTEGRATED ADMINISTRATIVE STRUCTURES

The Committee concurs broadly with the recommendations made in the Report of the Committee to Review the Existing Administrative Arrangements for Rural Development and poverty Alleviation Programmes (CAARD) in respect of integrated administrative structures for planning and development should be dynamic and independent and should at the same time be integrated with institutions of local self-government losing their dynamisms and independence.

The principal technical and administrative officers of various specialized departments along with their line formations should be part of the organizational and administrative structure of the Zila Parishad. The District Development Commissioner would be the Chief Executive Officer of Zila Parishad. The District Development Commissioner should be entrusted with the task of assisting in co-ordinating the planning and implementation activities of various departments, agencies and institutions at the district level.

Officers of high caliber, proven competence and sympathy for Panchayati Raj Institutions should be detailed to function as Panchayati Raj officials.

The Committee recommends that every official in the administration should be made to work in Panchayati Raj and rural development setting so as to sensitize our public administration to the problems of rural India.

The Committee emphasizes that the administrative structures should not be top-heavy and the administrative personnel should be made aware of the importance of Panchayati Raj Institutions and their accountability to them generally.

The Committee is strongly of the view that substantial training, research and public education inputs should be provided to strengthen the Panchayati Raj Institutions and the performance capabilities of those who are called upon to function as voters, elected representatives, administrative officials and voluntary workers in relation to Panchayati Raj Institutions. Voluntary institutions should be given the pride of place in providing these inputs. The Committee feels that this would be the most productive and profitable investment in democratic institution building.

A model legislation within the framework of the proposed new chapter in the Constitution should be prepared with sufficient scope for appropriate local adaptations.

The Committee recommends the National and State level local self-Government institutes, and Centres for training at the district level, should be established and entrusted with training, evaluation and research responsibilities particularly in relation to Panchayati Raj and urban local institutions. The institutes and centres should also be a clearing house of information relating to local self-government and should monitor and report developments in that field.

The Committee is of the view that the proposed National Institute of Local Self-Government should, in respect of its research and evaluation functions, utilize universities, research bodies and voluntary organizations such as All India Panchayats Parishad which should have a consultative nexus with it and which would be an invaluable resource for dissemination of information as well as for proper motivation

Source: Extracts from reports of various committees on PRIs, which appeared in *Kurukshetra,* Vol.XXXVII No.5, February, 1989. Main recommendations of these committees are given in the chapter-2 of the book.

Annexure-VI

Current Status in respect of constitution of District Planning Committees by various States & Union Territories in accordance with Ariticle 243 of the Constitution

A. States that have constituted District Planning Committee in accordance with Article 243 of the Constitution

States	Union Territories
1. Chattisgarh	1. Andaman and Nicobar Islands
2. Goa	2. Dadra and Nagar Haveli
3. Himachal Pradesh	3. Daman and Diu
4. Karnataka	4. Laksha-dweep Islands
5. Kerala	
6. Madhya Pradesh	
7. Manipur	
8. Rajasthan	
9. Sikkim	
10. Tamil Nadu	
11. West Bengal	
12. Assam	
13. Orissa	

B. Several State have not set up DPCs and their reasons for not doing so are indicated in table

S.N.	State	Latest Position and remarks
1	Andhra Pradesh	Andhra Pradesh had issued an Ordinance in September 2005 for the constitution of DPCs pending the passage of the relevant bill in the Legislative Assembly. The ordinance has now been replaced by legislation. Under the legislation, the Chaiperson of the District Panchayat is to be the Chairperson of the DPC. It has been reported that the elections to the DPCs will be completed by January 2007.
2	Arunachal Pradesh	It has been reported by the State that the composition and terms of reference of DPCs have been notified and that immediately after notification, they will be constituted.
3	Bihar	Bihar has laid down a calendar of events for the constitution of DPCs. Rules have been formulated for the same and are under vetting by the legal department.
4	Gujarat	Gujarat does not have a DPC but a nominated body, the District Planning Board, created through government order. It has been reported that draft legislation for the constitution of DPCs has been prepared and will be moved in the next session of the legislature.
5	Haryana	The Government of Haryana has decided to constitute DPCs in accordance with Article 243 ZD of the Constitution. The necessary rules and notifications are under issue.
6	Jharkhand	Since Panchayats have not been elected, no DPCs have been constituted.

7	Maharashtra	Maharashtra has a district level body, with equal representation from nominated members and elected representatives. A legislation for DPCs was passed, but has not been implemented so far. Rules have been published for inviting objections and after considering them if any, the rules will be finalized and will be followed by elections.
8	Punjab	Punjab has enacted legislation for the constitution of DPCs in October 2005. The conduct of DPC elections is under the consideration of the Government.
9	Tripura	In Tripura 70% of the area is under the 6th Schedule. There is a single tier system in ADC areas. DPCs therefore cannot be established through legal provisions in these districts. Tripura states that they have examined the issue from a legal standpoint and are in the process of creating DPCs through executive orders for the areas coming under Part IX of the Constitution.
10	Uttar Pradesh	Uttar Pradesh has enacted legislation for DPCs (in 1999), but is yet to issue the notification for the constitution of these bodies. They have a nominated body, the DPDC at the District level, which cannot be construed to be a DPC.
11	Uttaranchal	Uttaranchal, which inherited the UP Panchayati Raj Act, has also not notified or constituted the DPCs. The matter is under the consideration of the Government.

Union Territories

1	Chandigarh	Chandigarh has reported that since it consists only of one district and very soon the remaining villages in Chandigarh are going to be absorbed into the City, there may not be a need for the constitution of DPCs.
2	Pondicherry	Pondicherry is in a piquant situation because it has been exempted from the need to have a district Panchayat and have instead commune Panchayats at the intermediate level. A clarification is under issue to Pondicherry that the District Planning Committee may be constituted through election from amongst and by the members of the Commune Panchayats.

Souce: Grassroots Panning through Panchayats Chapter-V The State of Panchayats—A Mid-Term Review and Appraisal, Ministry of Panchayati Raj, Govt. of India November, 2006 pp. 78-79.

Annexure-VII

Constitution and objectives of Expert Group for Planning at Grassroots Level

This Expert Group was set up by the Ministry of Panchayati Raj vide its O.M. No. R 11017/17/2005 dated 10th May 2005 (as amended vide OM of even No. dated 14.6.2005) with the objective of studying and making recommendations on the following aspects of strengthening Panchayats in accordance with the recommendations of the Seven Round Tables:

a. Formulation of District and Sub-District plans at all levels of Panchayats aimed at delivering basic minimum needs to citizens at the grassroots level,
b. Strengthening the Planning Machinery at the district and sub-district levels for pursuing such formulation, including guidelines for the DPC to consolidate such plans,
c. Ways and means of strengthening the delivery system for services and development initiatives through Panchayati Raj Institutions,
d. Reviewing guidelines of centrally sponsored schemes and central sector programmes to ensure the centrality of participation by Panchayati Raj institutions from the drawing board to implementation of schemes including poverty alleviation, elementary education, rural health coverage etc.,
e. Development of model guidelines for conferring original jurisdiction on Gram Sabhas as envisaged in PESA.

Composition of the Expert Group

The composition of the Expert Group is as follows:

1. Shri V. Ramachandran, Former Vice-Chairman, State Planning Board, Kerala — *Chairperson*
2. Shri B.N. Yugandhar, Member, Planning Commission — *Member*

3. Shri D. Bandyopadhya, Former Secretary, Government of India, Ministry of Rural Development — *Member*
4. Smt. Nirmala Buch, Former Secretary, Government of India, Ministry of Rural Development — *Member*
5. Smt. Devaki Jain, Development Economist — *Member*
6. Dr. M. Govinda Rao, Director, National Institute of Public Finance & Policy — *Member*

In September 2005, the services of Shri T.R. Raghunandan, Joint Secretary, Ministry of Panchayati Raj, were made available as Secretary to the Group, in addition to his other duties.

Source: Planning at the Grassroots Level, Report of the Expert Group, Ministry of Panchayati Raj—Mach, 2006.

Annexure-VIII

Round Table: Schedule, Location and Subject for discussion

Date	Location	Subject for discussion
23rd and 24th July, 2004	Kolkata	Effective Devolution, comprising Functions, Functionaries and Finances, as well as empowerment of Gram Sahhas.
28th and 29th August, 2004	Mysore	Planning and implementation, including the question of parallel bodies; Rural Business Hubs.
23rd and 24th September, 2004	Raipur	"Reservations in Panchayati Raj", comprising Scheduled Tribes (including implementation of Panchayat Extention to Scheduled Area Act), Scheduled Castes and Women.
7th and 8th Oct., 2004	Chandigarh	Panchayati Raj in Union Territories; Panchayati Raj Jurisprudence.
28th and 29th October, 2004	Srinagar	Annual Reports on the State of the Panchayats (including pre-paration of a Devolution Index)
28th and 29th Nov., 2004	Guwahati	Panchayati Raj Elections and Audits.
17th, 18th and 19th December, 2004	Jaipur	Capacity Building and Training for Panchayati Raj Institutions, IT enabled e-Governance for Panchayats.

Source: The State of Panchayats—A Mid-Term Review and Appraisal, Ministry of Panchayati Raj, Govt. of India November, 2006.

Printed at Gopsons Papers Ltd, Noida